The Great Cover-Up

The Great Cover-Up

Joy Trachsel

DREAM YEAR

The Great Cover-Up: Inspiring Women To Be Real, Relevant & Ready
Copyright © 2013 by Joy Trachsel. All rights reserved.
ISBN 978-1-939676-04-7 (paperback).
Published by Dream Year.

All rights reserved. No part of this book may be reproduced or utilized in any form or by any means, electronic or mechanical, or by any information storage and retrieval system—except for brief quotations for the purpose of review, without written permission from the publisher.

Printed in the United States of America.

To my dad! I dedicate this book to the most creative man I have ever known. Thank you for being my ultimate protector, encourager and creative inspiration. We miss you and look forward to the day when we meet again in heaven! A light went out the day you died.

CONTENTS

Acknowledgments	9
Introduction	11
1: Uncovering the Problem	15
2: Uncovering the Gospel Within You	27
3: Uncovering Your Authentic Self	37
4: Uncovering the Sin that Binds You	47
5: Uncovering Your Passion	61
6: Uncovering Your Gifts and Talents	71
7: Now What?	81
8: Uncovering the Brokenness Near You - Bringing it Home!	93
9: Uncovering Your One	103
10: Uncovering Your Missional Entourage	115
Appendix: Stories of Passion	123

ACKNOWLEDGMENTS

To my heavenly Father I give you all my praise, honor and glory. It is only through your guidance that this book ever came to be. Thank you for your unconditional love and for allowing me to be the vessel to share this story. May the words in the book make you smile.

To my wonderful husband Wally and my amazing children (Ashley, Ally, Austin and Alex). I thank you for allowing mom to dream and withstanding many nights of pizza and takeout as I was busy making deadlines. You inspire me daily and I am so proud to be your wife and mother. May you always dream big dreams as you serve your big God.

To my West Virginia family for being my biggest cheerleaders! There truly is no place like home!

To my best friend Sandi who listened to me complain and proclaim many days of self-doubt. Thank you for being my Aaron when my arms grew tired and you held me up.

To my ministry partners, Carla Gasser and Jackie Judd, for your prayers and constant spurring on as I wrote the book. Thank you, Carla, for believing enough in the project to add the discussion questions for each chapter. I appreciate your passion for making women think and walking parallel with them through life.

Thanks to Ben Arment for being the ultimate guide for dreamers. Thanks for believing in me when self doubt and insecurity almost stopped me from writing this book. Please continue to inspire the dreamers who need a little shove. May CEO Joy always trump regular Joy.

I want to thank Janet Oberholtzer for being a source of encouragement and wisdom. You inspire me to never give up to always find ways to get over obstacles. ..."Because she can!"

Big thanks to the Dream Year publishing team for offering their personal and professional services. So honored to be one of the inaugural books from this great group.

Lastly, to the group of folks who were the first to say "We believe in you" by contributing to my Kickstarter campaign. You will never know what it meant! I adore all of you!

John and Amy Ridley, Kelly Pryor, Ruth Ridley, Meredith Mabus, Barb Corpora, Gay Yonkers, Mollie Dowdy, Lisa Leondarides, Guy Delcambre, Katherine Gillis, Anna Whitacre, Leigh Gray, John Finch, Tom, Ashley, Ally, Austin, and Alex, Jackie Judd, Andrea Leek, Mary Keller, Diana Kowalcyk, Karen Labbe, Marianne Richards, Carla Gasser, Sandra Horvath, Ginger Moore, Robin Toth, Kelly Norville, Pete Bruce, Jenni Pustinger, Aaron Foster, Laura Ridley, Julie Doll, Tom and Marilyn Schuck.

INTRODUCTION

My life was fine just the way it was. I was a stay at home mom to four wonderful children and was married to a wonderful man. I spent my days in the suburbs of Cleveland taking care of my family and driving my minivan to sporting events, endless practices and other commitments. I served at my church, attending numerous Bible studies and women's events. If you had a baby I always baked you a casserole and if you needed someone to sit with you at a doctor's appointment, I was your pal. I was your ideal Christian woman. I was a good person and was the epitome of a "good Christian." Remember the sketch that Dana Carvey did on Saturday Night Live called "The Church Lady"? Well, that was me, the good church lady that even lived behind a white picket fence. That was until March of 2010 when my world became unrecognizable. I will never forget the day my safe little Christian bubble burst.

I had spent the last two years as a substitute teacher (that is another book I should write someday) and was looking for a more permanent vocation. I had this romanticized idea of having a job that "mattered." I wanted to give back to others and began searching for a job at non-profits. I didn't care what it was—I was ready to hug a tree, save a whale, whatever it took to work for a social cause. I saw an ad for a homeless shelter that intrigued me and sounded like a good fit. Homelessness is a big problem in our world and maybe I could be part of the solution! I emailed my resume and then actually forgot about it.

On the fateful day, I was off work and not sure how I was going to spend my time. The following day I was scheduled to speak at an event in Akron, 35 minutes from my home, so I decided to scope out the location and prepare for the seminar. In ten years of speaking, I have never done this. But I got out of bed, threw on a t-shirt and jeans, put my hair in a ponytail and took off.

Ten minutes later my cell phone rang. It was a lady from ACCESS, the homeless shelter. I will never forget her words. "We received your resume and would love to interview you. Our schedule is very tight—what is the chance you could come to Akron?" After picking my jaw up, I replied, "You won't believe it but I am already halfway there." I went on to explain that I was dressed in jeans and a t-shirt but if they didn't mind, I would be happy to interview in twenty minutes.

I got out of my car and began to head into the interview until I realized I had a huge spaghetti stain on my shirt. This was in addition to being unshowered, with no make-up and my hair in a ponytail! I remembered the rain coat stashed in the back seat and threw it on, entering the shelter looking like a huge mess. I was a mess wearing a raincoat on a day with no rain. Everything was working against me. I laughed as I entered the building,

The Great Cover-Up

thinking if they hired me it either had to be from God or they were really desperate.

I am not sure which it was, but they hired me. However, despite my dreams of making a difference, I hated the job from the beginning. During the first two weeks, I went on three other job interviews! I begged God to get me out of there, informing Him this little social experience was over and I was ready to go back to my other life. You know...the one where I was comfortable... the one that didn't send me home crying.

The situations of the women in the shelter seemed hopeless. Their stories were sad and, well, I didn't *like* sad. I liked happy and fun. I liked hope and feel good. I didn't like stories about drug addictions, prostitutes, sexual abuse and hurting children.

One day one of those children asked me to play. I reluctantly agreed and walked to the playroom with her. She was an adorable child who was spending her formative years homeless and with an HIV+ mom. We began putting a puzzle together, and after twenty minutes had passed I looked in her big brown eyes and told her I couldn't stay any longer and we would have to quit the puzzle. She put her chubby little five-year old hands on each side of my face and uttered words that still haunt me today. "Miss Joy...never quit!" A little girl that was living in a homeless shelter and born to an HIV positive mom was telling me not to quit! That was all that I needed to hear. Ten minutes later we finished a life-size Barney puzzle, high-fiving each other as we celebrated our accomplishment. I returned to my office and she returned to her room. I am not sure about her...but I returned changed.

That encounter was more than just a story about two people in a homeless shelter, but it was a catalyst for this book. God showed me many things during those first weeks. He showed me what it means to be stretched for His purpose. He showed me what it looks like to be called and what it looks like to find your passion. More importantly, He showed me that being obedient is difficult and ugly and messy, but it's not impossible.

I am not sure where you are in your spiritual journey, but if you are ready to allow God to rock your world and use you in situations that are larger than you, then let's start this journey together.

If you are ready, turn the page. If you are not, turn it anyway.

CHAPTER ONE

UNCOVERING THE PROBLEM!

I hate Friday nights! Sounds odd, doesn't it? Let me explain.

I love my job at the homeless shelter so much there are actually days when I am not ready to leave. It's not because I'm drawn to the paperwork, emails and phone calls; it's that I'm drawn to the mission and the cause.

Each morning my frustration or exhaustion quickly evaporates when I walk downstairs from my office to grab my caffeine pick-me-up and engage with the women and children who call the shelter home. As I walk to the coffee maker, I pass addicts, felons, ladies struggling with mental illness and other women who call ACCESS home. I pass by children waking up to another day in a homeless shelter. Soon they will gather their backpacks and wait for the school bus in front of the building.

After pouring my coffee I return to my office invigorated and ready to work tirelessly to help these women and children. It isn't the coffee that energizes me; it's the people. It is their story, the look in their eyes, the human faces of poverty and injustice. It is the hope of possibly finding someone who can help us further our mission and the desire to see one of our women experience true change that day.

Each day as I turn off my office light and log out for the day, I leave with hope that maybe these dreams will be realized tomorrow. Maybe tomorrow affordable housing won't be so scarce and jobs will be offered so we can close the doors and go out of business. (I often wonder what our building would become if we could stop being a homeless shelter. I love the irony in thinking it might be a spa or a retail business.)

If a woman is still at the shelter on Friday, she will be there on Monday; rarely does anything change for a client over the weekend. Agencies that offer assistance are closed, staffs are smaller and hope is on hold for the weekend. There is always tomorrow, but not on Fridays.

At the end of each Friday there is almost a sense of defeat, knowing another week has passed and there is still a need for the shelter to exist. Each Friday night as I leave, there are always women standing outside for a smoke break. Walking to my car, I am haunted by "Have a good weekend, Ms. Joy" and "See you Monday, Ms. Joy!" I ponder the injustice of my weekend at home with family and friends, with the freedom to go where I want. I realize these ladies won't have a very "good weekend."

So for a while I hated Fridays.

Then I realized it's not Fridays I despise, it's the injustice of homelessness. If I worked at an orphanage, I would hate that a child is without a family for one more night. If I were employed at a battered women's home, I would hate the disappointment of a woman being out of her home one more evening as she nurses her wounds and disguises her bruises. In all its forms, I hate the injustice of the under-served and the overlooked and the marginalized of our society.

Scripture calls this group "the least of these." I call them my new friends. Scripture calls them the orphans and widows. I call them the lady who sat with me at lunch or the child who drew me a picture yesterday.

I often sit in meetings where politicians and social service agencies discuss the plight of the homeless and brainstorm ways to eradicate the problem with a ten-year plan. It seems we have taken this population and reduced them to statistics and demographics. I sit and listen and it takes all that's within me not to run out of the room and straight to the nearest church.

I want to storm into the pastor's office and shout, "WE NEED YOU!" I want to run to the next church and confront it with the 45 women and children who are living in a homeless shelter within walking distance of their steeple. I want to ask them to preach the command to serve others until every person embraces the call on their life and exhausts themselves for the Gospel.

I want to intrude on every women's Bible study within reach and beg them to help their sisters! I want to ask them to stop planning teas and potlucks and begin planning ways to walk alongside an overwhelmed woman in search of a job and housing. I am in no way bashing the church. Churches are doing amazing things to help the marginalized. But are we doing *enough*?

This is actually the proverbial "preaching to the choir." After all, I haven't always had this passion for the under-served. I am guilty of ignoring their needs and driving past them, passing judgment on what I assumed was their laziness. I am guilty of being too busy to stop and pray for a woman who is hurting or to offer a kind word to a broken sister. I am not leading this battle. I am searching just like the rest of you. But I do hope the homeless, the orphans, and the widows are not judging us. I hope they don't see us as "religious women" but that they see us as faithful women.

I wonder what the world would look like if we all found our cause. What would it look like if we all took the scriptures seriously and lived out the Bible with relentless obedience? I am not sure what it would look like, but I know it would look different! The world would look different, the church would look different and we would be different.

As I think about this I am reminded of the story of the Good Samaritan.

> On one occasion an expert in the law stood up to test Jesus. "Teacher," he asked, "what must I do to inherit eternal life?"
>
> "What is written in the Law?" he replied. "How do you read it?"
>
> He answered, "'Love the Lord your God with all your heart and with all your soul and with all your strength and with all your mind' and, 'Love your neighbor as yourself.'"
>
> "You have answered correctly," Jesus replied. "Do this and you will live."

But he wanted to justify himself, so he asked Jesus, "And who is my neighbor?"

In reply Jesus said: "A man was going down from Jerusalem to Jericho, when he was attacked by robbers. They stripped him of his clothes, beat him and went away, leaving him half dead. A priest happened to be going down the same road, and when he saw the man, he passed by on the other side. So too, a Levite, when he came to the place and saw him, passed by on the other side. But a Samaritan, as he traveled, came where the man was; and when he saw him, he took pity on him. He went to him and bandaged his wounds, pouring on oil and wine. Then he put the man on his own donkey, brought him to an inn and took care of him. The next day he took out two denarii and gave them to the innkeeper. 'Look after him,' he said, 'and when I return, I will reimburse you for any extra expense you may have.' Which of these three do you think was a neighbor to the man who fell into the hands of robbers?"

The expert in the law replied, "The one who had mercy on him."

Jesus told him, "Go and do likewise."
Luke 10:25-37, NIV

Jesus didn't just answer the question and stop. Instead, He ended with a mission. He told them to go. He explained it to them in terms they could understand and now they had no reason not to act. We must act as well. This has been explained to us and we need to "go and do likewise."

In the time it has taken me to write this book, I often asked myself, "Who is my neighbor?" Of course my immediate neighbors are the families who live beside me and across the street, but Jesus was asking us to think beyond the obvious and immediate. My neighbor is anyone who surrounds me. My circle is going to look a lot different than your circle, but I do know one thing for sure....WE ALL HAVE CIRCLES!

I have heard many messages on the number of evangelical Christians compared to the number of orphans in the world. I know that it is not possible for everyone adopt an orphan, house a homeless person and feed a family on an ongoing basis. But I believe we are all called to do something.

For some it will be a bigger sacrifice. For some it will be to adopt an orphan. For some it will be sponsoring a Compassion child. For some it may be bringing a family into their home. For some it may be providing pillows for a shelter. Do you know what that means to a homeless shelter? To you it may be a $10 investment—if thirty people did that each month, it would be a huge help. Let me say this: giving sacrificially can be addictive. . . just a warning!

How can we ignore the one who modeled this throughout the Bible? I am reminded of what He told the rich man:

> *Jesus looked at him and loved him. "One thing you lack," he said. "Go, sell everything you have and give to the poor, and you will have treasure in heaven. Then come, follow me."*
>
> *Mark 10:21, NIV*

He didn't say sell a few things, especially those things you no longer need. No. He said sell *everything* and follow me. Jesus talked throughout the scriptures of serving others and reaching out to those who have been overlooked and under-served.

He even compares it to planning a banquet.

> *But when you give a banquet, invite the poor, the crippled, the lame, the blind....*
>
> Luke 14:13, NIV

I remember feeling extremely honored when my husband and I were invited to have dinner at the Ohio Governor's mansion. I wanted to tell everyone. I wanted to buy the perfect outfit and make sure I had a photo to show all my friends... until I read this verse. Even though it was an honor to dine with the Governor, it doesn't compare to sharing a meal with someone who needs what only you or I can give. I would trade eating with kings and queens daily to be able to break bread with one soul who accepts Christ. I would rather dine with someone who needs what I can give than with a head of state or a Hollywood star.

I am so grateful I have a chance each weekday to eat with women and children who have been overlooked and under-served. There was a time in my life when this type of banquet would have been uncomfortable for me, a time when I would have sat beside them without partaking in the meal. I would have felt superior and awkward eating with someone who was homeless. I would have felt like we had nothing in common.

But a transformation took place. God softened by heart and revealed His truth, the truth that "set me free." He helped me break free from judgment and superiority, free from doing life my way and beginning to see that it wasn't about being good or doing good. He helped me realize that instead it was about doing what He has called me to do.

Join me and open your banquet table to those who deserve better. There is a whole world of hurting people. There is a city of broken lives within your reach. The world is not short on people in need. It is short on people willing to help with that need.

Let me repeat. If we are followers of Christ, it is not an option. It is an act of obedience.

Of course, even those who don't know the Lord as their personal Savior can do great things for the under-served. I believe anyone who chooses to give can help others. But those of us who have accepted Christ as our personal Lord and Savior are *called* to serve others. We should not be able to accept the injustice of the "least of these." It should light a fire within us that is so strong we can't help but react. Lastly, the genuine love for Christ and what He did for us should compel us to obedience.

We need to look in the mirror and ask ourselves what type of woman is looking back at us. Is it one who is true to her calling or one who is evading her mission? My goal for this book is for each of us to do whatever it takes to be the woman God has called us to be. It won't be easy and at times it won't be fun or pretty. It requires a heart that is searching for meaning and purpose according to God's Word. It requires a woman willing to prepare herself for the mission God has called her to. It requires a woman who will allow God to "search her heart" and reveal what is hindering her from her calling. It requires a woman who is ready to be authentic and real, a woman who is ready to explore and use her gift and talents, and a woman who is ready to say "yes" to God. We must be ready to uncover what needs to be uncovered. The time is now.

The title of this chapter asked "So what's the problem?" Some would say there is no problem. Some would say the problem is not *their* problem. Some would say the problem is too large and impossible to solve.

I would answer the question by saying this... the problem is us. The problem is we have focused on us more than on those in our circle of influence who are hurting and who need us. As Christian women who claim the scriptures to be the blueprint for our lives, we sometimes walk in an opposite direction.

Jesus was very clear when He spoke in the following scripture:

> *For I was hungry and you gave me something to eat, I was thirsty and you gave me something to drink, I was a stranger and you invited me in, I needed clothes and you clothed me, I was sick and you looked after me, I was in prison and you came to visit me.'*

> *Then the righteous will answer him, 'Lord, when did we see you hungry and feed you, or thirsty and give you something to drink? When did we see you a stranger and invite you in, or needing clothes and clothe you? When did we see you sick or in prison and go to visit you?'*

> *The King will reply, 'Truly I tell you, whatever you did for one of the least of these brothers and sisters of mine, you did for me.'"*
>
> Matthew 25:35-40, NIV

Reading the last verse should be enough to move us to serve the "least of these." Seeing our service as a reflection of how we serve Christ should be enough for us to live a "whatever it takes" mentality. To see the homeless, the poor, and the hurting as Christ should move us to act. To see the widow, the divorcee and the hurting neighbor in the same light as our Lord should energize us to serve.

So where do we begin? My prayer is that reading this book is a first step. I hope in some way it serves as a catalyst to a new way of seeing those who are hurting and in need of help. My prayer is that hearts will be softened and lives will be changed. Humbly I am also reminded that this book is merely words on paper that have no power. The true power only comes through the Holy Spirit dwelling within the reader. We must begin where everything that has meaning and value begins—we begin with Christ. We begin with the Gospel. If we allow the Gospel to transform us, there is nothing that can stop us.

DISCUSSION QUESTIONS:

1. Joy describes her journey as having her eyes opened to the injustice around her. Using a dictionary, define the words justice and mercy and discuss how they relate to helping "the least of these."

2. In this chapter Joy discusses the role of the church and believers. Reread the story of the Good Samaritan (Luke 10:25-37). What role do you think the church should play? How are you personally challenged to get involved?

3. Joy says we all have "circles." Make a list of the people in your circle right now. What specific things can you do to reach out to those people?

CHAPTER TWO

UNCOVERING THE GOSPEL WITHIN YOU

I will never forget Easter 2004. It was unlike any Easter I have ever experienced.

I cannot remember a time when my family did not celebrate Easter. I mean Easter from a biblical perspective, not a worldly perspective. When I was growing up, my parents did a great job teaching us the reason for the season. We knew it was more than Easter eggs and bonnets. We knew it was more than dyeing eggs and eating "peeps." We knew it was more than matching dresses, patent leather shoes and, yes, an occasional parasol. When I became a mom, I knew it was important to maintain this balance with my own children: exposing them to the Gospel and keeping them focused on the real reason for Easter while also allowing them to enjoy the traditions. When you are raised in a Christian home, it is so easy to get comfortable with both. It is easy to spend Easter with your feet in both worlds and feel okay with that.

But 2004 was a pivotal year, a year I allowed the Lord to truly penetrate my heart. It was a year when I was closer to God than I had ever been in my life. I felt true intimacy with Him and began to truly understand what it meant to have a personal relationship with Christ.

That year at our Good Friday service we watched a video depicting the crucifixion and brutal beating of Jesus. I had seen this video before. I had sat in the very same sanctuary checking the Good Friday service off my Christian to-do list. But this time it was different. I remember sobbing through the video. I remember almost physically feeling each brutal punch and whip. I remember actually jumping each time a soldier smacked Christ. I remember wanting to rush to the sound booth and ask them to turn off the video.

In previous years this had just been a video, but on this day it was a vivid reminder of what my Lord, my Savior, endured for me. It crushed me that my sin put Him there. I wanted it to stop. There, in this video, the Gospel was being played out. There, during this Good Friday service, the Gospel was being uncovered within me! For the first time, I felt like I was living parallel to Christ. I felt like I was being transformed by the Gospel, not just reading it or celebrating it, but being moved by it and changed by it!

Oh, praise Him!

I began to think. What just happened and why hadn't it happened before? What had I been missing until this "renewal" happened? I can justify this and say, oh, God's timing is perfect, but in reality, my timing is lousy. Or should I say my timing is lazy. The truth is, the Gospel was beginning to transform me. It felt amazing!

I accepted Christ into my life when I was six. Miss Marilyn told us about a man named Jesus, how He died on the cross for my sins and how He was preparing a place for me in Heaven. She explained in vague terms that if we accepted what He did and told Him we were sorry for the bad things we had done, we could spend forever in Heaven with Him. It sounded good to me, so I followed the rest of my friends and prayed the prayer Miss Marilyn prayed. I didn't feel different or look different but all I knew was I wanted to go to Heaven.

I spent the next 15 years of my life on a moral roller coaster, sometimes doing the right thing and many times not. I replayed the tapes in my head that I had heard as a child—ask for forgiveness and everything will be okay.

As I became an adult, I realized my problems were larger and I became more involved in the church. I began attending Bible studies and caring a little more for others and their needs. I began taking an occasional meal to people and every once in a while teaching a Sunday school class. I look back now and I am not sure of my motives—did I want to be more like Christ or like the more "spiritual" ladies in my church?

I followed this pattern until a summer mission trip in 2000. Oh, what a summer! The only way to explain what happened is to say I realized Jesus did more than just secure my home in Heaven. He gave His life as a ransom for mine and I needed to live a life that reflected that sacrifice. I also realized my salvation is not based on works, but my life needed to reflect my love for Him. I wanted to look more like Christ and start living with a radical obedience to His call.

In 2000 I was asked to go on my very first overseas mission trip. I will forever be deeply indebted to the people in Matamoros, Mexico. This trip was more about the way they ministered to me. My life was changed on that trip. It began when I was asked to do things I had never done before, like knock on the doors of strangers' homes and share my faith and walk around a city and pray. I was asked to do what I believe we all need to do: I was asked to leave my comfort zone and serve Him.

I had never shared my faith before and I wasn't sure I even knew how. I was so grateful for my interpreter. I asked him to feel free to change the interpretation if I said the wrong thing. But I quickly realized I just had to be willing to speak. God gave me the words and the courage, and eventually He allowed me to be part of lives being changed. I was sold out for Him! On the way home I prayed, "God…when I return home, use me the way you used me in Mexico." God was faithful in answering that prayer and continues to today. I desperately pray that He always gives me a heart like Isaiah. I want to be the kind of woman that cries out to God: "Lord, send me!"

I often wonder if we truly comprehend the Gospel. I wonder if we look at the "good news" as just a decision that one needs to make for eternity. It is more than my reservation for heaven—to me the Gospel is life. The Gospel is everything. Through Jesus' death on the cross He did create a way for me to have salvation from my sins. Through my acceptance of His sacrifice and my faith in Him, my future is secured. But it cannot end there. I cannot and must not only treat His death in a selfish manner and accept it as only my "ticket" to heaven. He desires my full surrender. He desires a relationship with me. He commands that I follow Him and He demands my obedience. It is unfair, unjust and selfish for me to believe that His death was only about my eternity and not to expect my life here on earth to be affected.

I was once asked to help someone prepare her testimony for a talk. She was not sure what to include and what to leave out, so I suggested she ask herself three questions: what was my life like before Christ, what contributed to my decision to accept His gift of salvation, and what does my life look like now? There needs to be a difference, inwardly and outwardly.

Even though you are reading this book, I am not going to assume you are a Christian or a follower of Jesus Christ. Because of my relationship with Christ and my desire to see His kingdom grow, I want to make sure I am faithful in what God has called me to do. But you need to examine *your* heart. Where are you placing your trust? Where is your faith?

If your faith is not in Jesus, then this book is just words. If you haven't acknowledged the amazing gift Christ offers us and accepted it as your own, the rest of this will be of no use to you. I beg you to ask yourself a very important question: "Have I accepted the Gospel and am I going to allow it to change all that is within me?" I pray that the answer is yes! If it is, let's hit the ground and get to work. If the answer is no or maybe, I hope you will contact me or another Christian you trust and be open, honest and transparent. Oh, how I pray that this book brings souls to Christ!

If we are truly allowing the Gospel to transform us, our lives will change and we will become more like Christ. D.L. Moody once said, "There will be three things which will surprise us when we get to heaven—one, to find many there that we did not expect to find there; another, to find some not there whom we had expected; a third, and perhaps the greatest wonder, will be to find ourselves there."

If we allow the Gospel to transform us, we will reflect a life that glorifies God and lives out His Word. No one should ever have to wonder whom we serve. The only wonder should be how they can have a similar life. Telling someone we are a Christian should not catch them by surprise.

I was born and raised in Charleston, West Virginia. Of four children, I am the only one who moved out of town. It is not uncommon for my mom to call me and give me updates on former classmates who still live in Charleston. I will never forget a time when she mentioned she had run into one of my close friends from high school. She was puzzled why my former classmate laughed when mom told her I was in full-time ministry at my church. That was hard to explain and disheartening to hear. I was a Christian in high school, but nobody knew!

Let me use marriage as an analogy. Imagine a bride and groom at the altar pledging their undying love for one another and to "forsake all others 'til death us do part." Days after the honeymoon, the bride informs her husband that from this day on they will just be roommates and all of the promises she made on their wedding day no longer matter. She promises not to ever divorce him because she likes the idea of being married but doesn't want to concern herself with the journey they could share together. All she cares about is being someone's wife.

So in this analogy, I purposely allowed the couple to have a honeymoon instead of severing the ties immediately. Why? Because I believe this happens many times after we give our lives to Christ. We accept Him and we are suddenly on fire. We are sharing the Gospel like it is the most amazing story we could ever tell. Then we go back to our old ways. Living the Gospel becomes harder and comes with resistance and even loss. We wonder why we should bother. I am going to heaven. Do I really need to do anything else?

If I allowed my marriage to become like the one just mentioned, I would only have a roommate and not a partner. I would have a friend but not an intimate partner. I would have companionship but often feel lonely. If I allow my relationship with Christ to become the same way, I am missing out on the blessings that come with an obedient walk with Him and the rewards that come with furthering His kingdom. I am missing out on an intimate walk with the "lover of my soul."

One of the greatest experiences I have ever had was leading someone to the Lord and seeing that person go from having no hope to having a faith in the One who offers peace, love and life. That experience trumps anything the world can offer. I love telling others about Jesus. I yearn for more invitations to speak at events where the Gospel is shared, where people attend expecting to hear spiritual truths.

Then there is the other part of my life, working at a government-supported homeless shelter. Being surrounded by brokenness and feeling muzzled by not being allowed to talk about my faith is indeed frustrating. It is so hard to look at these women and not want to just shout from the roof that Jesus is Lord and He can restore you and carry your burdens. It's like seeing someone dying and knowing that you have the cure but are unable to offer the medicine. I respect the rules but struggle with the limitations.

In other words, I hate being told that I am not allowed to do something that I so desire to do.

I know I can't be stopped from praying for the women and children who live at our shelter, but the activist in me desires to be proactive. It took me a while to realize I did have ways to take the Gospel to this under-served population. I began to seek out churches that would come to the shelter and host Bible studies and spiritual events. Clients could voluntarily sign up and not be forced to attend. I am so grateful for the churches that are faithful in serving at the shelter to sometimes an audience of one or two.

I also realized that I was missing an important facet of the Gospel that Jesus modeled on a regular basis. He loved others. He "did life" with unbelievers. He shared love without even using words. He modeled relational evangelism. I could show the clients the love of Christ by serving them, loving them and walking beside them. I finally found my method, and the journey has been amazing and tiring. It has been rewarding and draining. It has been all about allowing the Gospel to compel me to serve them and not quit.

Sometimes the opportunities come when it is not convenient, when I am busy and at my worst. I recently represented ACCESS at a fancy affair. It was a great evening speaking on behalf of the women and children who call our shelter home. At the end of the evening I felt a conviction to return to the shelter. It was a nudging that was so strong I could not ignore it. My aching feet were crying for me to go home, but the other urging won.

When I walked into the shelter I saw a cab leaving. I asked who was leaving and was told one of our clients was being rushed to the hospital. The staff member went on to tell me how scared the client was to go alone. Yes, it was clear what God was asking. He was asking my husband and me to follow her to the ER. I had never met this client, so I was trusting God would let me know who she was when I entered the waiting room; I was concerned the hospital would not identify her due to confidentiality issues. But when I walked into the waiting room I immediately knew who she was. It wasn't because her appearance stood out or because she looked poor. No, she was the only one sitting alone. All the other patients had a loved one with them for support. She was alone!

If we call ourselves followers of Christ, if we have committed our lives to being conformed to His image and we are aware of someone walking a desperate journey alone, we will be there. If we allow the Gospel to resonate and not lay dormant within us, we will be compelled to go out and make a difference. There will be no stopping us!

The longer I work at the shelter, I realize I have more in common with the ladies than I expected. We are all moms who love our kids, and sometimes only one decision separates me from them—a decision regarding a relationship, a decision to numb the pain with a drug, a decision to drop out of school. We need to realize their circumstances don't define who they are. It doesn't make them less of a person. They deserve the best. They deserve a second chance and they deserve to hear the Gospel through authentic and genuine believers.

DISCUSSION QUESTIONS:

1. Joy describes a time in her life when her relationship with Jesus had become routine; where she was just going through the motions of being a follower of Christ. Have you ever felt that way? Explain.

2. Briefly write down your own faith story asking yourself these questions:
   - What was my life like before Christ?
   - What contributed to my decision to accept His gift of salvation?
   - What does my life look like now?

3. Look up these verses and discuss how you would use these verses to share Christ with someone.
   - 2 Timothy 1:9-10
   - Mark 8:35
   - Romans 1:15-17

CHAPTER THREE

DISCOVERING YOUR AUTHENTIC SELF

I love speaking at women's events. I love hanging out with women of all ages. I enjoy those who are on Twitter and those who are on Medicaid. I enjoy those who are on Facebook and those who are getting facelifts. You get the picture! I especially look forward to speaking at retreats, with several days of "escape"—two or more days of women acting like they haven't been away in years and escaping for fellowship, food and fun.

It is almost inevitable that each session begins with an icebreaker. Confession time…I am not a fan of these games. Please don't ask me to find someone else with blue eyes who was once a cheerleader or dreamed as a teen that they would marry Donny Osmond. (I had to throw the last one in as a tribute to all of us who remember his purple socks and can still sing all the lyrics to "Puppy Love.") I find it awkward walking around trying to guess the name of the person someone has taped to their back. But if we have to do an icebreaker, there is one I sometimes enjoy—the purse scavenger hunt. You know the one…there is a list of items and you try to see how many you can find in your purse.

I almost always win. In fact, often before the retreat begins I will fill my purse with odd items in case we play this game.

You can tell a lot about a woman by what she carries in her purse. If she has diapers and sippy cups she is probably a mother of small child. If her purse contains 100-calorie snack packs, she is probably on a diet. And if her purse contains a battery-operated fan and an ice pack, she is probably enjoying the pains of menopause!

Yes…you can tell a lot about a woman by what she has in her purse, including myself. In fact, my purse says a lot about who I am and who I am not. If you looked in my purse you would learn I am a fake, phony and a fraud. My purse does not support who people think I am. OUCH! That is hard to admit— how can I talk about being authentic if I am not willing to be transparent myself?

As I prayed about this chapter I had mixed feelings. I asked myself if it was really necessary for me to blow my cover. Was it necessary for people to know so much about me? The answer to both was yes!

Let's break this down. First there is the driver's license. I know many of us tend to take liberties with our personal information at the DMV. Why not? They don't make you step on a scale. What harm is there? I mean it's not against the law. You can add me to the group of people who lie about their weight.

Why? I hate the struggle that I have with my weight. For me to be honest about my true weight would mean that I would have to acknowledge the number. I am not the weight on my license.

If you dig a little deeper, you will see piece of paper with a number that keeps me awake at night, a number that requires me to work outside the home and makes me a "slave to the lender"—my credit card statement. This happened because of another lie. I was trying to be someone I was not and own things I could not afford. For several years now I have realized the importance of paying off this debt and owning who I am and who I was designed to be. I used to take great pride when people complimented me on my nice clothes and jewelry or when they would ask to borrow a purse or accessory. What I desire now is for my heavenly Father to shower me with blessings for honoring Him. That trumps any earthly compliment.

This next one is the hardest and most humbling. I love encouraging people or helping them see the positive side of a situation. Most people would consider me an extrovert who likes to have fun. But this wasn't always the case; for years I have been battling depression and ongoing anxiety. I can let fear overcome me in a moment. I can let fear take me to a place where happiness seems unattainable.

It became really bad about five years ago. My emotions were all over the place and I assumed it was hormones and would eventually balance itself out. What I didn't see were the consequences for my family. One particular evening my emotions took over and hurtful words came freely out of my mouth. I ran upstairs to my room and threw myself over my bed. A name popped into my head. I wasn't sure why; we were only acquaintances at church. Maybe I was supposed to call her and ask her to pray for me. I dialed her number and asked her to pray for me. She asked if I would mind telling her what was wrong.

I could hardly get the words out through my tears. Once I finished she quietly said, "I understand." She began to share her battle with the same issues. She comforted me, encouraged me, prayed for me and even offered to go to the doctor with me. She gave me hope and information, but even more importantly she gave me a private piece of her authentic self. I did go to the doctor and was put on medication. For two years I was able to manage the symptoms and have since been able to go off the medicine. But to this day I still carry the refill with me. I know I am prone to this condition and I never assume I am totally cured. As I dig in my purse on the constant search for a pen or gum, my hands will often stumble onto that bottle. It is a constant reminder of a dark time in my life, a time when I wasn't who people thought. It is a constant reminder that I haven't always been happy, calm and peaceful. It is a reminder that I haven't always been who people think that I am.

Until now, I have been afraid to tell people about my struggle with anxiety. I was afraid they might judge me or think that I lack faith. I remember once I was giving a talk on authenticity and in the middle of the talk, God asked me to tell my story. As my hands became sweaty and my mouth dry, I spoke the words I felt ashamed to share. After the session, a dear young mom approached me with tears in her eyes. She thanked me for sharing my story and began to share her own. We cried and prayed together and then I thanked God for asking me to be authentic. I praised Him for nudging me and I thanked Him for allowing me to help another woman.

Why do we pretend? Why do we try to be something or someone we are not? It is exhausting to live a lie, and there is no purse large enough to carry around all of the masks we wear.

Trying to be something you are not can also be uncomfortable…and humorous.

I was preparing to speak to a large group of about 400 women. As I tried to decide what to wear, nothing fit. Everything was too tight. Well, whose fault is that? Then I remembered something I had bought for "such a time as this." (Okay...I know that Esther reference was inaccurate but I couldn't resist!)

I had bought a pair of Spanx! Have you seen these? Have you ever tried to put them on? It must resemble the process of making sausage links. By the time I squeezed into them, I could barely walk and was miserable—but I looked smaller.

At the venue, I began to really doubt my decision when the sound tech asked me, "Joy, where will you be attaching your microphone piece?" What! Umm....I think I will go in the bathroom and take care of this, if you don't mind.

The event began and I was introduced. I began to take slow, small steps to the stage, because the weight of the microphone was causing my Spanx to slide down with each step. I like to walk around when I speak, but that night it was not to be; I stood behind the podium like a soldier. I was miserable. I was frustrated. I got through the night without incidents or injuries, but what a lesson I learned. First...never buy irregular Spanx at an outlet store. And second...be who you are.

There are two vital truths. First...we cannot serve God unless we are authentic. What does that mean? The dictionary defines it as "not false or copied; genuine; real." Hmmm...that pretty much sums it up...doesn't it?

Have you ever heard a group of teens excitedly exaggerating something until one of them suddenly says "Get real"? We all need to take that advice and "get real." No one wants to put their trust in someone who is fake or full of it.

As we search scriptures, there is evidence that an authentic life is desired by God.

Blessed are the pure in heart, for they will see God.
                                                Matthew 5:8, NIV

For the Lord searches every heart, and understands every desire and every thought.
                                        1 Chronicles 28:9b, NIV

I love how each scripture contains the word "heart." Our heart is what drives our physical body to stay alive and also what drives our "spiritual existence" to be healthy. It is easy to hide ourselves since often we are the only ones who know the truth. But as the scriptures make clear…God knows! I think it is comical how designers create handbags with outrageous price tags and then someone comes along and creates a knock-off. They can fool many people, but the original designer can always spot the "fake."

Most knock-offs will have one subtle flaw separating them from the original. What a great parallel to us! Sometimes it may be only one thing in our lives…but that one thing can create a gap in our relationship with God. Ever tried walking with a tiny pebble in your shoe? It is extremely painful. It is not the size of the sin…it is that fact that it is sin!

We also cannot serve others without being authentic. As women, we have probably heard the story of Esther many times. Many teachers use the story to talk about obedience and beauty, but I've often thought there is a character in the story who is overlooked—Queen Vashti.

The Great Cover-Up

> *On the seventh day, when King Xerxes was in high spirits from wine, he commanded the seven eunuchs who served him—Mehuman, Biztha, Harbona, Bigtha, Abagtha, Zethar and Carcas— to bring before him Queen Vashti, wearing her royal crown, in order to display her beauty to the people and nobles, for she was lovely to look at. But when the attendants delivered the king's command, Queen Vashti refused to come. Then the king became furious and burned with anger.*
>
> Esther 1:10-12, NIV

Can you imagine the scene? There has been a banquet going on for seven days that involved many men drinking. The Queen is summoned to come and stand before this drunken group and allow them to ogle her. She said NO! Way to go Vashti! But if you continue to read the story you will learn she faced consequences and her life changed dramatically. She had standards and values and this request was not in alignment with them. We learn a great lesson from this former royal. Being authentic may sometimes come at a high price.

I have spent most of my professional life in ministry, mainly working with volunteers. I enjoy working with those who want to give back and have an enthusiasm for the mission. The rest, as far as I am concerned, should just stay home. This sounds harsh and insensitive but there is a reason for my feelings. Let me explain. I receive phone calls daily from people who want to volunteer at the shelter. Some want to volunteer because they have a true desire to serve and support the cause of homelessness. I have also seen people come to the shelter with their own agenda.

A red flag always goes up when I hear them say, "I want to work directly with the homeless." This may not seem tragic to you, but here is what I really hear them saying: "I need a warm and fuzzy experience with someone who is less fortunate so I can go away feeling good about myself and then I will post pictures on Facebook and add a status update that makes everyone cry and think I am Mother Theresa."

This happens often at the shelter. I am not saying the request itself is bad, but the motives may be. Come to the shelter with humility and a willingness to do whatever is needed. Come for the clients, not the photo op. Come the other 11 months of the year and not just the ones that involve colored eggs, turkeys and eggnog. Don't let the spirit of the season direct your serving…let the spirit of the One who saved you direct your steps. Homelessness doesn't take a holiday! (Officially stepping off my soapbox now.)

Don't pity them…help them. Don't feel sorry for them… feel empathy and compassion for them. Don't make them your cause…make them your peer.

I love the volunteers who come to our shelter on a regular and ongoing basis. They are the ones who have the chance to develop relationships and see the value of investing in the long term. Volunteers, like the ones described above, are committed and help us to further our mission. They model the value of being faithful by making it a priority and not something they just "fit" into their schedule. As an employee of a homeless shelter, I have seen the value of being faithful in this commitment and being authentic in our approach. It is no secret that some of our clients can be difficult at times. Much grace is given to them as we try to understand their situation and the frustration that one feels when they are homeless. Being homeless is not a natural state of being and is hard to overcome today. It is always encouraging when we see a woman who is determined to overcome her crisis and get back on her feet.

I am honored to call one of those ladies a good friend. I met this woman when she was a client at ACCESS. To protect her confidentiality, I will call her "Grace." Grace was homeless by choice; she lived in a homeless shelter because it was better than living in a home that was dangerous, immoral and unsafe. Grace was always happy and was an encouragement to everyone. She worked hard to find a home and ran into one obstacle after another.

It was great to get to know Grace outside the shelter. We were able to talk openly about spiritual topics and about our lives. I remember opening up to her one time and telling her about a very difficult time in my life. I will never forget when she said, "Miss Joy...I never would have guessed that you went through that." It was a pivotal time in our relationship. I was no longer the shelter employee and she was no longer a client. We were just two friends having coffee, two women who had gone through some hard times. We were equals. It served as a reminder that the ground is level at the cross. He died for me...and He died for her. He loves each of us the same even though one was homeless and one lived on a cul-de-sac.

You want to serve God and others? Find your authentic self and be ready for the next step.

DISCUSSION QUESTIONS:

1. Think and pray about the things that may be holding you back from your authentic self. Write these down and give them to the Lord today. If you cannot think of anything specific, spend some time in prayer asking God to reveal them to you.

2. Read the following verses about the truth and explain what the Bible says about those who seek truth and those who do not.
   - John 8:32
   - 1 John 1:8-9
   - Psalm 15

3. Joy says we cannot truly serve God or others unless we are willing to be genuine and authentic. Do you agree? Explain why.

CHAPTER FOUR

UNCOVERING THE SIN THAT BINDS YOU

Let us throw off everything that hinders and the sin that so easily entangles, and let us run with perseverance the race marked out for us. Let us fix our eyes on Jesus, the author and perfecter of our faith, who for the joy set before him endured the cross, scorning its shame, and sat down at the right hand of the throne of God.
Hebrews 12:1-2, NIV

Addiction is a nasty thing! In the 18 months I've worked at the shelter, I have heard more about it than ever before. There are addiction classes, addiction training, and addiction support groups. The bottom line is addiction is why half of our women are homeless. Addiction is why children live there with their moms. Addiction is causing newborns to live in a homeless shelter. Addiction is why a teen gets ready for the prom at a homeless shelter. Addiction is why two-year-old twins learn ballet for the first time at a homeless shelter. Addiction is why Christmas presents are opened and stockings discovered at a homeless shelter.

When I first began to work at ACCESS, I felt like a fish out of water. It wasn't just because of the work being done and the clients we served, it was also about the staff. Many of the employees had struggled with their own addictions and they seemed to have their own vernacular. They would talk about counseling the clients and use terms that were foreign to me. They seemed to be able to relate to the clients on a deeper and more personal level. When they looked into the eyes of a mom battling alcohol, they could honestly say to her, "I understand what you are going through" and mean what they were saying. I could not. My replies were in vague terms of very little substance. They were being authentic and transparent. I was just being nice. Their words had hope and a face behind the recovery. Mine were short and unmeaningful.

I soon realized God gives each one of us our individual trials we can use to encourage others. He spared me from battling an addiction, but He chose other circumstances for me to overcome. It is not so much the kind of battle He can use, but our willingness to be an obedient warrior in the fight. It wasn't my lack of an addiction that made me feel inadequate, it was my sin of pride and comparison to others.

The longer I work around women in crisis, the more I am totally blown away be their tenacity and resilience. The ones who succeed are overcomers and go-getters who are willing to put their pasts behind them and move on. They don't let their history dictate the future or let their sin get in the way of their mission.

Hope is one of those women. Hope's story could make an Oscar winning film. Let me introduce you to this resilient woman. She is in her late forties, tall and loved by everyone. She has a unique way of correcting you and praising you without you even knowing the difference. She is street smart and head smart at the same time. She is an inspiration. I met Hope shortly after I began working at the shelter.

It didn't take me long to realize Hope had a past before she had a Saviour. But now, Hope had a new life in Christ and in recovery. As I watched Hope move about the shelter, she spoke openly about both. One was her past, while the other was her future.

As Hope learned she could trust me, she began to share stories of her past. Hope would not say she WAS an addict. She said, "I AM an addict." She helped me realize that once an addict....always an addict. She shared how a large part of her life was about finding her "drug" and how this addiction took over her life and family. She shared stories of the extreme measures she went through to score her next high and the danger that came with that.

I knew Hope trusted me when she showed me her "scar." In her before-recovery life, Hope made bad decisions, and a few even left physical scars. She didn't see the scars as a sober reminder of her past, but a positive reminder of battles she had fought and overcome, battles that were fought on her knees through prayer. Christ was with her through the addiction and sustains her through recovery, but although her wounds healed, they left a scar. I thought to myself...how unfair is that? Hope's reply shows you her spirit. She didn't see this as unfair or let it define her. Instead, it serves as a reminder of who she was and who she prays she will never be again.

Hope's addiction caused her to become homeless. She had nowhere else to go so she made the decision to come to ACCESS Homeless Shelter. Hope no longer lives at ACCESS; she is employed and is in stable housing. She loves bragging about ACCESS and is grateful for the time she spent in the shelter. Hmmm….sounds odd doesn't it? That someone would ever say they were grateful for living at a homeless shelter? Looks like Hope also realizes the command to be "joyful" in all things. This lady truly is a walking example of God's word and faithfulness.

Hope's story inspires me each day when I feel inadequate, overwhelmed and unqualified. I am all of those things, but I'm reminded in His word that through Christ, I am also a new creation, beautiful, filled with God's Spirit, not forsaken and deeply loved beyond measure.

Hope's story also reminds me I have choices as I face struggles and discouragement. I can give into them and accept defeat, or I can be like Hope. She realized the following two things as she worked though her addiction and homelessness:

1. The stronghold that sin can have on us.
2. How it can keep us from living a full life for Christ.

Hope's story is different than what we sometimes see at the shelter. Over 65% of our women come into the shelter because of an addiction. Some of them will refuse to take any steps that will move them closer to sobriety and permanent housing. They won't acknowledge their problem and their need for help. Yes, they might call themselves an addict and say they want to be healed and transformed, but their actions do not support this. Hope did and her life changed. They won't, so their life stays the same, sort of like the proverbial hamster on a wheel. Doing the same thing over and over only gets you to the same place...over and over.

When it comes to dealing with our sin, I believe Hope's life models what Christ does for us if we allow Him. I like to call this the three R's: Christ reveals our sin to us, He calls us to repent and He restores the relationship with Him and others.

In John 4 Christ gives us an amazing model of this very process with the Samaritan woman.

> *The Pharisees heard that Jesus was gaining and baptizing more disciples than John, although in fact it was not Jesus who baptized, but his disciples. When the Lord learned of this, he left Judea and went back once more to Galilee.*
>
> *Now he had to go through Samaria. So he came to a town in Samaria called Sychar, near the plot of ground Jacob had given to his son Joseph. Jacob's well was there, and Jesus, tired as he was from the journey, sat down by the well. It was about the sixth hour.*
>
> *When a Samaritan woman came to draw water, Jesus said to her, "Will you give me a drink?" (His disciples had gone into the town to buy food.)*

The Samaritan woman said to him, "You are a Jew and I am a Samaritan woman. How can you ask me for a drink?" (For Jews do not associate with Samaritans.)

Jesus answered her, "If you knew the gift of God and who it is that asks you for a drink, you would have asked him and he would have given you living water."

"Sir," the woman said, "you have nothing to draw with and the well is deep. Where can you get this living water? Are you greater than our father Jacob, who gave us the well and drank from it himself, as did also his sons and his flocks and herds?"

Jesus answered, "Everyone who drinks this water will be thirsty again, but whoever drinks the water I give him will never thirst. Indeed, the water I give him will become in him a spring of water welling up to eternal life."

The woman said to him, "Sir, give me this water so that I won't get thirsty and have to keep coming here to draw water."

He told her, "Go, call your husband and come back."

"I have no husband," she replied.

Jesus said to her, "You are right when you say you have no husband. The fact is, you have had five husbands, and the man you now have is not your husband. What you have just said is quite true."

"Sir," the woman said, "I can see that you are a prophet. Our fathers worshiped on this mountain, but you Jews claim that the place where we must worship is in Jerusalem."

Jesus declared, "Believe me, woman, a time is coming when you will worship the Father neither on this mountain nor in Jerusalem. You Samaritans worship what you do not know; we worship what we do know, for salvation is from the Jews. Yet a time is coming and has now come when the true worshipers will worship the Father in spirit and truth, for they are the kind of worshipers the Father seeks. God is spirit, and his worshipers must worship in spirit and in truth."

The woman said, "I know that Messiah" (called Christ) "is coming. When he comes, he will explain everything to us."

Then Jesus declared, "I who speak to you am he."

Just then his disciples returned and were surprised to find him talking with a woman. But no one asked, "What do you want?" or "Why are you talking with her?"

> *Then, leaving her water jar, the woman went back to the town and said to the people, "Come, see a man who told me everything I ever did. Could this be the Christ?"*
>
> John 4:1-29, NIV

I LOVE THIS STORY! It is by far my favorite story in the Bible. First, I love how we don't know the woman's name. (I call her Joy.) I love how Christ breaks with tradition as He ministers to this woman. As a Jew, as a religious leader and as a man, it would not have been customary for Him to even be speaking to a woman, let alone a Samaritan woman. Jews hated Samaritans! But Christ didn't let culture and prejudices stop him from seizing the moment to save a life.

One of my favorite parts of working at the shelter is seeing lives changed. Sometimes it is the client, and sometimes it is the volunteer. The latter is what makes my heart jump! I have seen women of faith come into our shelter to volunteer and be nervous about what they might experience. During their first visits to the shelter, they spend most of their time at arm's length from a homeless woman. But then transformation takes place. After several visits, their arms begin to extend and begin to embrace the ladies physically and emotionally. They start to realize a homeless woman is just like them except for not having a permanent place to live. She is not dirty, mean and dangerous. She is feminine, gentle and pleasant.

I visualize this Samaritan woman at the well alone. Most women came to the well early in the day while it was not hot. Scripture says she came around noon when the heat would have been at its worst. I'm guessing she came then because she didn't want to be there while the other women were. Maybe she was ridiculed for her lifestyle and shunned by the other women. She wasn't one of them…she wasn't like them. Sounds familiar? Maybe the others kept her at arm's length and it was just easier to be alone. She probably awoke thinking this was going to be just another day…but oh how she was wrong. This ordinary day became an extraordinary day because of a man who broke tradition and engaged her in conversation.

We see that Jesus engages her in conversation about water. Instead of coming at her with a guilt-driven conversation, he approaches her on a level she can understand. How many times have we not stopped to help someone or to engage a hurting woman in conversation because we didn't know what to say? What if we just followed the model of Christ and met them where they were instead of expecting them to meet us where we are? What if we removed what I like to call the "ication" words (sanctification, justification, etc.) and spoke non-Christian rhetoric like love, grace, mercy, etc. Let's try to make God famous and not ourselves.

Through this conversation Jesus reveals the sin in her life. He confronts her about her past relationships and her current one.

We see through this dialogue that she does have some sort of spiritual foundation and teaching. She had been taught that there will be a Messiah, but had no idea that she was standing face to face with Him at this moment.

We can also learn another important thing as we see Jesus chat with this woman. A dialogue needs to be a two-way conversation. It was important for her to ask questions and receive answers.

As a parent, there are times when I need to confront my children regarding bad choices. If I choose to tell them what they did was wrong with no reason or explanation I have failed as a parent. One time, one of my children had made a bad choice regarding a friend. As a parent, I had the right to tell him they couldn't be friends, but I needed to tell him why. How else would he learn not to choose that friend again? I want my children to know they can ask me the "why" and not get in trouble. It is also okay to ask God "why" but we have to be ready to accept the answer. This story reminds us He is willing, even eager, to be in dialogue with us.

We see further into the chapter that Christ calls her to repentance and then ultimately to restoration.

> *Many of the Samaritans from that town believed in him because of the woman's testimony, "He told me everything I ever did." So when the Samaritans came to him, they urged him to stay with them, and he stayed two days. And because of his words many more became believers. They said to the woman, "We no longer believe just because of what you said; now we have heard for ourselves, and we know that this man really is the Savior of the world."*
>
> *John 4: 39-42, NIV*

After this pivotal conversation with Christ she returns and saves an entire village. WOW!!! To think that a woman they once shunned now captivated their attention. Wonder what that tent meeting was like? I believe the village responded because they saw a difference in her and because of the movement of the Holy Spirit. It was the right person sharing the right message at the right time.

Hope models this idea perfectly. She was once shunned by society because of her addiction, but now uses her past to heal others. Christ took both the woman at the well and Hope and used them in a mighty way.

That is my prayer for everyone who reads this book but it is important to remember that we are nothing without Him and we can only lead a person as far as we ourselves have been. If we are being held back by our sins, we are useless to God.

We see another example of Christ's compassion and His desire for us to reveal our sin, repent and be restored in John chapter 8. We have often heard this story referred to as the woman caught in adultery. Oh how I love that she is also un-named!

But Jesus went to the Mount of Olives.

At dawn he appeared again in the temple courts, where all the people gathered around him, and he sat down to teach them. The teachers of the law and the Pharisees brought in a woman caught in adultery. They made her stand before the group and said to Jesus, "Teacher, this woman was caught in the act of adultery. In the Law Moses commanded us to stone such women. Now what do you say?" They were using this question as a trap, in order to have a basis for accusing him.

But Jesus bent down and started to write on the ground with his finger. When they kept on questioning him, he straightened up and said to them, "If any one of you is without sin, let him be the first to throw a stone at her." Again he stooped down and wrote on the ground.

> *At this, those who heard began to go away one at a time, the older ones first, until only Jesus was left, with the woman still standing there. Jesus straightened up and asked her, "Woman, where are they? Has no one condemned you?"*
>
> *"No one, sir," she said. "Then neither do I condemn you," Jesus declared. "Go now and leave your life of sin."*
>
> John 8:1-11, NIV

The only one who could deal with this woman's sin was Christ—not the religious teachers, the Pharisees or the village. It was his role…not theirs. He revealed the sin, called her to repentance and restored her. And what He did for her, he can do for you and me!

Do you want to be a woman God can trust with big things? If so, you must deal with your sin. A prideful woman cannot bring a humble message. A materialistic woman cannot teach the message of "dying to oneself." A gossip cannot show unconditional love to the lost.

Of course, we don't have to be perfect to be used by God. That will never be possible until we are in heaven. But I do believe we need to have a sincere desire to follow Christ wholeheartedly and not let our sin get in the way. This will be an ongoing struggle and one we will not be able to overcome on our own. We must have a genuine desire to seek His guidance and grace as we become more like Christ.

I am reminded of how gold becomes more precious as it is refined in the fire. Let's humble our hearts before our King and ask Him to search our heart, and even put it "through the fire." This process creates the humility of a genuine servant.

If we are women who humbly ask God to "search our hearts," we are taking an important step to conform ourselves to His image. Clearing away the "yuck" isn't fun, but what follows is amazing—we will be able to let our passions be revealed and serve Him wholeheartedly.

DISCUSSION QUESTIONS:

1. Reread either the story of the Samaritan woman (John 4:1-42) or the story of the woman caught in adultery (John 8:1-11). Identify how Jesus reveals the woman's sin, calls her to repent, and restores her.

2. Read Psalm 139:23 and write it out on an index card. Post it in a place where you can see it often throughout the day. Ask God daily to reveal your sin, then confess it and repent. Journal your experiences.

CHAPTER FIVE

UNCOVERING YOUR PASSION

It was supposed to have just been a trip to Africa. It was supposed to have been a chance to speak at a woman's conference and then return home to a regular life. It was supposed to have been an opportunity to pour into some women and minister to them. God had a different plan!

The above sentences describe an experience my ministry partner Ginger Moore had in 2010. Ginger and I ministered together on a team called Speaking Thru Me. One does not have to be around Ginger very long to realize she has a passion for three things: God, speaking and orphans. It is a great thing when multiple passions collide and that is exactly what happened to Ginger.

She was invited to go to Liberia and participate in a conference for the women of Africa. A chance to minister through speaking and to hug the necks of Africa's orphans was an invitation she could not resist. A woman named Celia traveled eight hours to hear the message. She was desperately seeking something she prayed Ginger could provide. She was looking for hope.

After the session Celia found Ginger and begged for her help. This mother had a baby who was severely ill. She was born with a condition that is rare and confusing to their villagers. Basically all of her internal organs were born on the outside of her body. Her village had shunned her and thought this child was demonic. She was counseled to let the child die. She received no help or support from her community. Being a woman of faith, she knew there was hope—she just needed to find someone else who shared her belief. She found the right person at the right time when she found Ginger. She came to the event armed with the only medical records she had. Celia handed them to Ginger, a complete stranger, and begged Ginger to help her. The decision was not hard at all—it wasn't a question of if she was going to help, but of how!

After returning home to Nashville, Ginger began to pull together a network of prayer partners, financial partners and medical partners. Within months she had secured all of the money, medical resources and travel arrangements needed to bring Celia, her daughter Dolly, her husband and a translator to Nashville. Within months Dolly had surgery, recovered and returned home a healthy baby. With God's leading and power Ginger followed her passion and made a difference in many lives. Watching her live out her faith touched the hearts of many, including mine. There were stories after stories of God's provision through this experience. Ginger's faith and passion were both tested and both prevailed.

Can you imagine what the world would be like if we each found our passion? Can you imagine how many more orphans would have homes if everyone who confessed to have a passion for orphans acted like Ginger? Could you imagine if everyone who had a passion for those in poverty followed through on their conviction? If we each lived out our passion we would look like the church God desires.

> *Your very lives are a letter that anyone can read by just looking at you. Christ himself wrote it—not with ink, but with God's living Spirit; not chiseled into stone, but carved into human lives.*
> 2 Corinthians 3:2-3, MSG

A passion is something that energizes, angers or moves you to act and is allowed to inconvenience you. The above story completely describes what a passion looks like. Ginger has a passion for orphans. Just talking about the forgotten children fills her with a contagious enthusiasm. It angers her to see so many children without a home and she is called to action, even if it means leaving the comforts of her home and traveling abroad. She allows this cause to inconvenience her and doesn't wait for conditions to be perfect before she acts.

The word passion can be used in flippant ways. Even in the coldest winter months you will see fans passionate about their sports teams. They will endure frigid temperatures and conditions to watch their team play. Fans of musical groups will camp out for days in order to secure a ticket to a concert. I believe it is healthy for us to have interests and hobbies that help us escape from our routine…but I believe we have to ask ourselves an important question: what am I doing to further the kingdom?

> *Whether you turn to the right or to the left, your ears will hear a voice behind you, saying, "This is the way; walk in it.*
>
> Isaiah 30:21, NIV

What is your passion? Is there something in your life that energizes you, causes you to want to act and is allowed to inconvenience you? I am talking about something beyond your family and loved ones; hopefully we would all say we are passionate about our relationships. I am talking about something that needs your attention and response and is bigger than yourself and your everyday.

I am passionate about three distinct things: speaking to women, advocating for those who are experiencing homelessness and/or poverty, and evangelism.

How do I know this? I know it because of the questions that I asked earlier. Spending time with women and teaching or speaking about spiritual issues energizes me. Sometimes the night before a speaking engagement feels like Christmas Eve. I LOVE IT! It's not that I am an amazing speaker....it's because God has given me a joy about speaking and has removed the fear. Don't get me wrong, I still get nervous before I am about to speak and make numerous trips to the restroom. I don't enjoy the spiritual attacks that come before and after an event but I know it is expected and draws me to my knees. Preparing for a message forces me to dig deep into God's Word and the prep time is a sweet time with God.

I have a passion for the homeless because the injustice puts a fire in my belly to do more. It compels me to advocate with all that I have and to bring their cause to the minds of others.

I know I have a passion for evangelism because I earnestly pray that God will bring others into my life who need to hear the good news. I will allow evangelism to alter my day or my schedule if needed. As I write this chapter of the book it is almost time for bed. I don't want this day to end because today, June 14, 2011, my passions collided. I spoke at a women's luncheon and shared about the homeless shelter and Jesus. WOW! Christmas in June.

When I think of people in the Bible who had passion, Paul stands out.

Paul's conversion experience was unbelievable. To say that Paul did a 180 is an understatement! He was once a man who sought out Christians to kill and destroy them, but we later see him as one of the most prominent and radical evangelists of the New Testament. A man who once hated Christians was proclaiming the message with a passion. He became one of those he had once despised and hated. His passion to kill Christians was replaced by a passion to further the kingdom.

Paul's passion was his faith. It energized him and helped him endure months of strenuous travel and dangerous conditions. The bad behavior and idolatry of others angered him and it moved him to preach that much harder. Paul allowed his passion to inconvenience him to the point of imprisonment, health issues and death threats. He endured much for his passion.

I believe it is the people with passion who change lives, change conditions and ultimately change the world. The opposite of passion is complacency. Which do you want to be? Which do you think God wants you to be?

> *"Not that I have already obtained all this, or have already been made perfect, but I press on to take hold of that for which Christ Jesus took hold of me. Brothers, I do not consider myself yet to have taken hold of it. But one thing I do: Forgetting what is behind and straining toward what is ahead, I press on toward the goal to win the prize for which God has called me heavenward in Christ Jesus."*
>
> *Philippians 3:12-14, NIV*

In the next chapter we are going to talk about gifts and why it is important for us to realize how we are gifted (and how we are not). The same could be said for passion. For example, if everyone had a passion for orphans, who would advocate for the sex trafficking epidemic? If everyone had a passion for addiction issues, who would advocate for the mentally challenged?

Passion cannot be forced upon you…it has to be your own and sometimes our passions change. For many years my husband and I worked in youth ministry. It was fun serving together, but after awhile I felt like God was calling me to women's ministry. I fought the call for some time. I didn't want to let go of the overnight retreats, the mission trips and the never-ending supply of ice cream. I knew it was time to make the switch when it began to drain me. The fun times were easy but preparing to teach teens and finding creative ways to make a spiritual point began to frustrate me. When I transitioned to women's ministry I felt my energy return.

My mom has a different story. She spent many years staying at home raising three well-behaved and adjusted children (and then she had me). Once we were grown and more independent my mom found her passion—teens. She began to work at a high school and fell in love with helping teenagers who were under-served or what she had labeled the "underdogs." I have seen my mom leave the comfort of her bed in the middle of the night to rescue a teen. I have seen her counsel a young teen about to have an abortion. I have seen her go to dangerous parts of town to make sure a teen went to school. I have seen her buy prom gowns and shoes so a teen could attend prom. I have seen her life be interrupted for a teen and be energized through the process. I see my mom live out her passion today at the age of 72 and she shows no signs of stopping.

I also think of Carl and Laura Rarlston. This amazing couple have dedicated their lives to eradicating the use of children in the sex trade business. This mission and passion began at a conference. Just a normal non-eventful conference...that turned about to be life-changing for Carl. A speaker at the conference began to tell stories of young girls who had been lured into this terrible world. One story stood out to Carl. Nhu was a 12-year-old girl who had given her life to Christ. Her family did not approve of her conversion from Buddhism to Christianity and sold her into the sex trade business. The fact that she was a young virgin made her even more desirable. The speaker was unable to share with the crowd how the story ended. This moved Carl to not only make sure this did not happen to other innocent children, but also to find Nhu.

Carl and Laura began a journey that would eventually lead them to find Nhu and make her part of their family and ministry. The Rarlston family sacrificed many things and moved their life overseas to be "hands-on" in this ministry.

Carl and Laura were moved by a cause. They could have easily written a check, prayed a quick prayer and washed their hands of the need…but that is not what passion does. Passion moves us to give wholeheartedly, serve willingly and love unconditionally. Passion causes a restlessness inside us until we say yes. Passion moves us to do what seems odd to others, but normal to a child of God.

The demented world of sex trafficking has one less victim because of Nhu. Carl and Laura can't save them all…but they can save some.

Let me close by saying that passion may last only a season, but it needs to last longer than a moment or it is just a hobby. When I was in junior high, I remember having a new crush each week. Each week I was madly in love with a new boy, passionate about each crush until the new one came along. It can be the same with our passion. We are on fire for something until a new cause comes along and distracts us. Sometimes when our "passion" becomes too hard we look for another issue that may look easier or more fun.

Passionate people have found their cause and are courageous. Passionate people are obedient. Passionate people are contagious!

DISCUSSION QUESTIONS:

1. What is Joy's definition of passion in this chapter? Do you agree? What would you add to her definition?

2. Do you know what your passion is? If so, explain. If not, what steps can you take to go about discovering it?

CHAPTER SIX

UNCOVERING YOUR GIFTS AND TALENTS

When my son was about six, he excitedly told me, "Mommy, I know exactly what I want to be when I grow up—a professional soccer player!" A million thoughts went through my mind. First, there was the practical side of me that thought, "No way." This was coming from a child who spent most of his time looking at the dandelions on the field and not the ball! He was not showing any of the great talent that one needs to be a professional athlete. Second, I assumed this was a fleeting desire that would soon be replaced by the desire to be a fireman or a power ranger. Finally, there was the response I chose to share with him. I stooped down to his level, looked him in the eye, and said, "Austin…you can be anything God wants you to be!"

He ran off, since little boys never walk, and returned to his life of dreaming and not practicing soccer. Fast forward almost ten years. Austin is now a teenager with a different dream, one that suits his skills and gifts. He is a very talented musician and plays in the worship band. He also excels at baseball. You see, he didn't need me to shatter his childhood dreams, and that was not my responsibility. My responsibility is to encourage him to dream while always pointing him to the Dream-giver. I knew that if each one of my children walked closely with God they would realize their gifts, talents and ultimately their God-given dream. I also know that what God calls them to do, He will equip them for.

Sometimes as adults we give advice to our children on this topic but we fail to listen to it ourselves. I'm grateful I have a family that has allowed me to go through this process even as an adult. They supported my dream of opening a decorating business and lived with my creative experiments. They supported me when I began to have home parties peddling cookware and kitchen gadgets (although I hardly ever used them at home). And they supported me when I had the crazy idea to write this book. As I type they are allowing me to spend an evening writing while they eat carry-out. I am blessed with a family that supports my dreams and blessed to serve a God who equips me for the dream. This same God is available to each of you as well. He has entrusted you with talents and expects you to use them for the kingdom.

Pertaining to our giftedness and talents, scripture is very clear that, as believers, we are each given a gift.

> *Now about spiritual gifts, brothers, I do not want you to be ignorant. You know that when you were pagans, somehow or other you were influenced and led astray to mute idols. Therefore I tell you that no one who is speaking by the Spirit of God says, "Jesus be cursed," and no one can say, "Jesus is Lord," except by the Holy Spirit.*

There are different kinds of gifts, but the same Spirit. There are different kinds of service, but the same Lord. There are different kinds of working, but the same God works all of them in all men.

Now to each one the manifestation of the Spirit is given for the common good. To one there is given through the Spirit the message of wisdom, to another the message of knowledge by means of the same Spirit, to another faith by the same Spirit, to another gifts of healing by that one Spirit, to another miraculous powers, to another prophecy, to another distinguishing between spirits, to another speaking in different kinds of tongues, and to still another the interpretation of tongues. All these are the work of one and the same Spirit, and he gives them to each one, just as he determines.

1 Corinthians 12:1-11, NIV

The bottom line is this: we all have gifts and we are all called to use them! But how do you know what your gift is?

One option is a spiritual gift test. If you have never had a chance to take one, I encourage you to do so. But be honest and don't answer the questions the way you *want* to be or the way that seems most "spiritual." God created you the way you are!

You know what I mean...remember in high school when we had to take those dull career assessments? I remember not answering the questions honestly so the results would show that I should be something exciting like a rocket scientist or master gardener.

Another option, and the one I think is best, is to ask the people closest to you. Earnestly pray for God to reveal your gifts to you and ask yourself what comes easy to you. Then ask someone you trust what they think, and be open to their answer.

I would love to sing. I truly wish I had an angelic voice, but I don't—just ask the person who sits in front of me at church. That's okay. God has created all of us differently. If we all had the ability to sing gloriously, the choirs would be full and the audience would be empty.

As you seek to realize your spiritual gift for this season of your life, it is important to be ready for God's response. I have often seen women fight their natural giftedness because they want to serve in an area that brings more affirmation and attention. I have seen women who have the gift of administration desire to speak and it is painful to see this struggle. Most speakers and teachers will tell you that they did not search the limelight as they began feeling called to speak. It was a battle that they fought with no peace coming until they said yes. We have to "yield" ourselves to God and allow Him to direct our paths. It is only with humility that we will be mold-able and effective with our talents. Our job is to make God famous…not ourselves. Discontentment can come on this journey if we are not careful.

It is beautiful to see a group come together with different gifts and talents. Like a detailed puzzle, no two pieces are alike, but without each the picture is incomplete.

As I look at the staff of ACCESS, I see an amazing example of God equipping each of us with a special talent in order to work toward the mission of the homeless shelter. The shelter has two distinct departments; the client service department serves the homeless women and children through case management and advocacy, and the business side of the shelter handles operations, finances and administrative support. In the short time I have been employed at the shelter I have had the opportunity to work in both areas. One area drained me and the other energized me.

During my brief stint as child advocate I loved working with the children and moms…for a short time. But after just a few hours of intervening with angry children and stressed moms, I found myself craving solitude and time in my office. Case management would be left undone as I desperately tried to find duties I found less stressful.

I was later transferred to another department that fit my talents. I now spend my days advocating for the women as the Public Relations Coordinator. It allows me to use the gift of speaking God has given me and gives me the opportunity to be their voice. I love it! It energizes me. If the shelter only hired staff members gifted in social services, our clients would receive amazing care with no funding. If they hired only business-minded staff, we would have a strong donor base and good financials but our clients would not receive the support they need. Both groups are vitally important.

Imagine this scenario: a dear friend calls a group of women to share the news of a recent breakup. Each woman has a unique way of ministering to her. The woman with the gift of exhortation will cheer her up and tell her what a great girl she is and that someone better will come along. The woman with mercy will offer her a shoulder to cry on and some chocolate. The woman with the gift of hospitality will begin to organize a party and the woman with the gift of administration will research all of the single guys in the church and make sure they are invited. Let's not forget the prayer warrior who will awake in the middle of the night to pray for her while the one with the gift of helps will already be at her house throwing away his pictures and presents!

This story may be an exaggeration, but it illustrates how different people can use their gifts to serve. It is evident how important this topic is when one sees the many scriptures devoted to it. And if it is important to God, then it must be important to us.

I received a phone call at the shelter from a woman who wanted to bring a group of ladies to volunteer. This is not an unusual occurrence, but this time it seemed a little different. I asked her a question that I don't often ask: "Why?" Sounds strange, doesn't it? I mean, most nonprofits are so desperate for volunteers and assistance that sometimes the "why" doesn't matter. She explained they had recently done a Bible study on the popular book "Crazy Love" by Francis Chan. The book moved them and they knew they had to act and allow the book to change them. They wanted to continue to meet as a group but wanted to be active and put what they had learned into action. They decided to do a lesson one week and a service project the next. They wanted to invest in a cause and commit to the project. They selected ACCESS as their project and wanted to bring the group for a tour.

When the group arrived I gave them the usual tour and took them upstairs to talk. So far, this group was like many others that have visited the shelter. They cried over our cause and asked what they could do. We decided on a project and made arrangements for them to return in two weeks.

When the group returned they immediately jumped into the project of redecorating a lounge for our clients. What happened next was remarkable. Each lady took on a task that fit her gifts. One of the women was gifted in administration; she organized the group and the plan. Several of the women used their gift of exhortation as they encouraged some of our clients. Some of the women prayed with our clients and a few even spent time with our clients outside of the shelter.

God designed this group exactly the way it was needed. If He had sent us 12 volunteers with the gift of administration, the work would have been organized in a great way but never completed. If He had sent us a group of women with the gift of mercy, our ladies would have been ministered to but the work would have gone undone. All of the gifts were important and all of the gifts were needed. This group was a great visual of what God intends for the church.

> *The body is a unit, though it is made up of many parts; and though all its parts are many, they form one body. So it is with Christ. For we were all baptized by one Spirit into one body—whether Jews or Greeks, slave or free—and we were all given the one Spirit to drink. Now the body is not made up of one part but of many.*
>
> *If the foot should say, "Because I am not a hand, I do not belong to the body," it would not for that reason cease to be part of the body. And if the ear should say, "Because I am not an eye, I do not belong to the body," it would not for that reason cease to be part of the body. If the whole body were an eye, where would the sense of hearing be?*

If the whole body were an ear, where would the sense of smell be? But in fact God has arranged the parts in the body, every one of them, just as he wanted them to be. If they were all one part, where would the body be? As it is, there are many parts, but one body.

The eye cannot say to the hand, "I don't need you!" And the head cannot say to the feet, "I don't need you!" On the contrary, those parts of the body that seem to be weaker are indispensable, and the parts that we think are less honorable we treat with special honor. And the parts that are unpresentable are treated with special modesty, while our presentable parts need no special treatment. But God has combined the members of the body and has given greater honor to the parts that lacked it, so that there should be no division in the body, but that its parts should have equal concern for each other. If one part suffers, every part suffers with it; if one part is honored, every part rejoices with it.

Now you are the body of Christ, and each one of you is a part of it. And in the church God has appointed first of all apostles, second prophets, third teachers, then workers of miracles, also those having gifts of healing, those able to help others, those with gifts of administration, and those speaking in different kinds of tongues. Are all apostles? Are all prophets? Are all teachers? Do all work miracles? Do all have gifts of healing? Do all speak in tongues? Do all interpret?

1 Corinthians 12:12-30, NIV

This journey of finding your gifts and talents can be both exciting and frustrating. Pride and envy can get in the way as we try to be like someone else. I remember when my daughter Ashley was in sixth grade and wanted to be a cheerleader. She was excited and we supported her in this endeavour. As a former cheerleader, I knew a little bit about what would be expected from her at tryouts. I watched her practice numerous times and realized cheerleading was probably not her sport. As a mom, I wanted to encourage her to try new things but I also wanted to protect her heart from hurt and rejection. I was stressed on the day of tryouts and dreaded seeing her heartbroken if she did not make the squad. Tryouts came and went and we did not add a cheerleader to our family. But I was happily surprised when her reaction was the opposite of what we had expected. There were no tears of sadness and no hours of locking herself in her room. On the contrary, Ashley bounced back quickly and decided to move onto a new challenge—cross country. She was a natural and went on to run in high school and college. Cross country helped pay for her education and is still a passion she has as an adult.

Ashley found what she was good at—and what she wasn't. It didn't mean she didn't have to work hard at the sport, but her passion gave her strength for the journey.

Isn't it amazing how God brings us together to work together to further His kingdom?

DISCUSSION QUESTIONS:

1. Go online and take a spiritual gift/inventory test. Be honest! What are your spiritual gifts? Are you surprised by any of them? Explain.

2. Describe a time when you saw a group of people using their unique gifts to accomplish something for God's kingdom. What did it look like?

CHAPTER SEVEN
NOW WHAT?

If you work long enough at a homeless shelter, you begin to see patterns. People are homeless because of addictions, because of chronic bad choices in relationships, and because of their own choices. But sometimes the pattern is broken. It was broken recently at ACCESS.

I was walking through the commons area of the shelter when a little boy caught my eye. He was about 12, well-dressed, and quiet but there was something about his eyes. They weren't just sad...they looked scared and lonely. I just stood and watched him from a distance. I began to talk to his grandmother, who said she was homeless due to the economy. She was close to retirement and now had custody of this boy. They both lived in the shelter but she was very motivated and was trying to fit in her meetings before her grandson had to leave for his baseball game.

What? This precious young boy has to prepare for an important ball game at a homeless shelter? I was quickly reminded of my two sons who love baseball. They lay out their uniforms the night before and get plenty of rest before the big game. Not this little boy. He has to accompany his guardian to countless meetings at the shelter before joining his team at the game. He prepares for the game at a homeless shelter while his teammates get ready at home.

No boy should get dressed for his little league game at a homeless shelter. No girl should prepare for a dance recital at a homeless shelter. No teen should get ready for prom at a homeless shelter. Bottom line…no one should have to do anything at a homeless shelter.

We have neglected the least of these. I think we have forsaken Christ's teaching and turned it into the "least of me" for the least of these. I think to sit idly on the sidelines as hurting people cross our paths is selfish. I think it is arrogant to assume we are not called to help.

Each day I walk by women who are living in the shelter and ask myself what brought them here and who let them down. Many believe homeless people are lazy and don't want to have a better life. That may be true for some, but why did they adopt that attitude? Was it modeled by their parents?

Let me ask you the "what ifs." What if someone had intervened in that lady's life before her circumstances forced her to become homeless? What if we had made ourselves available to someone who needed us? What if we were obedient to God's Word and let Him do the directing?

God's word is not vague on the idea of serving the least of these. We just ignore the simple command to GO! Simple…but not easy. Uncomfortable….but not impossible.

Let's examine this journey together.

I believe we do nothing for three reasons:

We are selfishly judgmental.

We are selfishly distracted.

We are selfishly fearful.

OUCH!

You may think doesn't describe you. Well, I am confident it describes ME! Let's break this down.

We are judgmental.

If we were honest with ourselves, we would admit we are very judgmental when it comes to others…especially women. You don't have to go far to see examples of this on television and in real life. For a brief time I was a substitute teacher and often taught in elementary schools. It amazed me when I would see girls as young as kindergarten being judgmental of each other. How does this start so early? Is it learned by others or by the older influences in their lives? I don't have the answer to those questions; I just know it starts early and only grows.

Why are we so hard on each other?

Of course the obvious answer is the sinful nature that lives within us. We can't use that as an excuse when we have a heavenly father that promises to walk through this struggle and to equip us to overcome this character flaw. This judgmental attitude is obvious when it comes to the women we serve at ACCESS. Volunteers and potential donors often come in with a preconceived idea of why they are homeless. At times it angers me to see this attitude, but then I remember I once had that mindset, too, and it changed only by learning about the cause and getting to know the women. I believe that is the answer. Before we place judgment…why not take that energy and get to know the person or the cause.

Scripture cautions us in this area.

> *For by the grace given me I say to every one of you: Do not think of yourself more highly than you ought, but rather think of yourself with sober judgment, in accordance with the measure of faith God has given you.*
>
> Romans 12:3, NIV

I truly believe our judgmental attitude is really a reflection of our own self-worth and insecurity. We feel lousy about ourselves so we bring others down with us. How often have you muttered, "It could be worse…I could be like so and so"?

We are distracted.

I went through a tough time recently and my oldest daughter was brave enough to call me out on it. She reminded me that if Satan can't stop you he will distract you. In this case I was distracted by fear and worry about my business. How many times have we been so focused on ourselves and our lives that we drove by the person on the side of the road?

Jim Elliot once said, "Wherever you are…be all there." As women we brag about our abilities to multi-task. We wear it as a badge of honor that we are able to wash dishes while we talk on the phone, or plan a holiday party while driving to work, or apply mascara while driving on the freeway. When did busyness become the new normal? At times I'm so busy that sitting still seems awkward. I don't want sitting still to seem odd. Scripture says we need to be still.

Be still, and know that I am God; I will be exalted among the nations, I will be exalted in the earth.
Psalm 46:10, NIV

A few years ago I was heavily involved in ministry activities as well as serving on several committees. Somehow I felt all this busyness gave me status and credibility. It was Christmas time and I had been working with the children's Christmas program. It was the day of the big performance and I felt a sense of accomplishment and pride as the children took the stage. I took a moment to scan the crowd and saw my family sitting a few rows behind me. I wondered who the little girl was sitting with my family and realized IT WAS MY SON! His hair had grown so long that it was combed to the side and looked like a little girl's hairdo. WHY? Well, I was so busy doing ministry that I had neglected my son's hair. He was way overdue for a haircut but I was much too busy helping those who seemed more important. This story is funny now, but still a reminder to me when I am tempted to be distracted from what is important. (And yes…we did invest in a haircutting kit.)

I have learned the value of saying no and not feeling guilty. I believe that outside of the essential things that we must do, we must have a standard of what we say yes to. Hmmm…something to consider…something to prayerfully consider. I am reminded how Jesus was always taking time to minister to others. Nothing was more important than that. He allowed himself to be interrupted and inconvenienced. Ministry was a lifestyle to Him and should be to us. When an opportunity arises for you to help someone...we need to respond. Why don't we?

Ever had a discussion with a younger child pleading with you to do something that so far has resulted in your "no"? You end your conversation with the all-important and many times overused..."because I said so." Well...your ABBA father says so... and that should be enough. But...it's not. We want reasons and details.

Are you ready to step away from your judgment, remove your distractions and throw aside your fear? If the answer is yes, then keep reading! If the answer is no, you just wasted your money and you are missing something that is much bigger than yourself. I am saddened that you are not willing to partner with the creator of the universe and be part of something amazing. I am heartbroken that you don't see that we can't do everything but each can do something.

Let's begin this journey!!

Since the terrorist attack on September 11, 2001, we have been made more aware of the armed forces and the special units that are trained for specific tasks. These troops weren't just handed a uniform and a weapon and told, "Go fight this war." Some of my friends are married to soldiers serving in Afghanistan and they have shared how grueling the training can be. These soldiers train for months and sometimes years under intense stress and scrutiny. The army wants only the best on the front lines. They want the soldier who has done everything to prepare himself for battle and service. An inexperienced and unprepared soldier is useless for their purposes.

An unprepared servant can be just as useless to God. The first part of this book focused on God's call on your life and your preparation to serve Him wholeheartedly. Consider the first six chapters "boot camp." Now we'll talk about another important component: God has a mission for you and it is not to sit and do nothing.

Sitting in the comforts of your church pew is not an option. Sitting back and closing your eyes to the hurting and broken people of the world is selfish and sinful! It is not a choice for a Christ-follower. Why? God said so!

Writing this book came through the assistance of a program called Dream Year. Ben Arment, the founder, took 24 of us through the process of identifying our dream and helping us navigate the process. One of the things Ben encouraged us to do was make the big "asks." In other words, ask for things that were sometimes hard and made us feel uncomfortable. I believe that God has the ultimate Big Ask....to follow Him and be obedient.

> *Then the eleven disciples went to Galilee, to the mountain where Jesus had told them to go. When they saw him, they worshiped him; but some doubted. Then Jesus came to them and said, "All authority in heaven and on earth has been given to me. Therefore go and make disciples of all nations, baptizing them in the name of the Father and of the Son and of the Holy Spirit, and teaching them to obey everything I have commanded you. And surely I am with you always, to the very end of the age.*
>
> *Matthew 28:16-20, NIV*

The poor and the broken were important to God and they should be important to us. If we truly want to be like Christ, then what breaks His heart should break ours. We don't get a pass to serving the broken.

> *He will reply, "I tell you the truth, whatever you did not do for one of the least of these, you did not do for me."*
> *Matthew 25:45, NIV*

We are fearful.

It is sad that we let fear stop us from doing amazing and incredible things. It starts early as a child is afraid to take the training wheels off his bike. As we mature the fears become worse and harder to overcome. Fear is a great tool Satan can use to stop us from being obedient to Christ. It paralyzes us and can render us ineffective. We listen to our fear while ignoring the voice of the One who matters.

Read the following passages and let them resonate within your heart for a moment.

> *Do not be afraid, little flock, for your Father has been pleased to give you the kingdom.*
> *Luke 12:32, NIV*

> *For God did not give us a spirit of timidity, but a spirit of power, of love and of self-discipline.*
> *2 Timothy 1:7, NIV*

> *God is our refuge and strength, an ever-present help in trouble.*
>
> Psalms 46:1, NIV

> *When you pass through the waters, I will be with you; and when you pass through the rivers, they will not sweep over you. When you walk through the fire, you will not be burned; the flames will not set you ablaze.*
>
> Isaiah 43:2, NIV

I don't know about you, but I want to exhaust myself for the cause of Christ. It is simple to write those words, but there are many times I have contemplated quitting ministry. Sometimes the spiritual battle is just too hard. Sometimes it just seems easier to take the easier road…the path of least resistance.

But I am so grateful that when I find myself in the valley, I know who I can call. I have friends who won't let me whine and excuse myself from my calling. They speak truth into me and encourage me to keep on. Do you have friends like that? If you don't…find them!

We need to realize He is not going to call us to do anything He is not going to equip us for. Didn't He equip Noah to build that ark? Didn't He give Esther everything she needed to risk her life for her people? Didn't He walk with Mary when He told her she would be carrying His son? The Bible is not just a book of stories. The same God who parted the Red Sea and turned the water into wine is your God and my God. That power exists today for us. The Bible is full of men and women who witnessed the amazing, transforming power of God.

I often refer to Isaiah when I am looking for a role model in this area.

> *In the year that King Uzziah died, I saw the Lord, high and exalted, seated on a throne; and the train of his robe filled the temple. Above him were seraphim, each with six wings: With two wings they covered their faces, with two they covered their feet, and with two they were flying. And they were calling to one another:*
>
> *"Holy, holy, holy is the LORD Almighty; the whole earth is full of his glory."*
>
> *At the sound of their voices the doorposts and thresholds shook and the temple was filled with smoke.*
>
> *"Woe to me!" I cried. "I am ruined! For I am a man of unclean lips, and I live among a people of unclean lips, and my eyes have seen the King, the LORD Almighty." Then one of the seraphim flew to me with a live coal in his hand, which he had taken with tongs from the altar. With it he touched my mouth and said, "See, this has touched your lips; your guilt is taken away and your sin atoned for."*
>
> *Then I heard the voice of the Lord saying, "Whom shall I send? And who will go for us?"*
>
> *And I said, "Here am I. Send me!"*
>
> *Isaiah 6:1-8, NIV*

Isaiah said yes—and God said GO!

I want to be like Isaiah. Isaiah didn't say "maybe" or "let me think about it." No…he was hearing from God and he knew there was no other option. Are you ready to utter the words of Isaiah? He has already said GO…we just need to say YES!

DISCUSSION QUESTIONS:

1. Joy claims there are three reasons we do nothing when it comes to serving "the least of these": we are judgmental, distracted and/or fearful. To which of these do you relate to most? Explain why.

2. The Bible gives several commands in relation to serving. Joy reminds us it is not an option, but an act of obedience. Look up the following verses—Matthew 22:37-39, Luke 6:32-36, John 15:12-17—and discuss what it "looks like" to truly follow Christ. Be specific!

3. Reread the story of Isaiah and his response to God in Isaiah 6:1-9. Are there things holding you back from saying yes to God? Write them down and give Him those things today!

CHAPTER EIGHT

UNCOVERING THE BROKENNESS NEAR YOU – BRINGING IT HOME!

Have you ever lived next door to someone in sales? If you have, you would know. Most seasoned and successful salespeople who are passionate about their product will not miss an opportunity to make a sale. We have always lived in neighborhoods where families knew about each other's lives and yes, I have even lived beside a few neighbors in sales. In a very respectful way, they made their services available and were not pushy. When a time came for us to need their particular service, we called upon them. However, a few years ago my husband and I had friends who were pretty high up in a direct sales business. The basis for success in this type of business is to recruit other people to join and you begin to earn money off of their success. We were around this couple quite a bit but they never approached us about the opportunity. I remember thinking, "What is wrong with us? I'm sure they are constantly on the lookout for future partners— why don't we fit the bill?" I wondered why they asked other acquaintances but not some of the people closest to them.

Why do we sometimes treat sharing the Gospel and serving others the same way my friend approached his business plan? We will be the first to sign up for a mission trip in a tropical location, but have never shared Jesus with our family or our neighbors next door. We will pack a duffel bag and board a plane, but we won't walk across the street. We will volunteer to be on every church committee while we have family members in desperate need of a Savior.

A missionary recently came to our church to share about his ministry. I assumed this would be the usual presentation complete with PowerPoint slides of tribal members, stories about eating strange food and a plea to give money and prayer support. But his talk was anything but predictable. The missionary shared briefly about his ministry but then he went a direction that was not expected. He began to share that many people romanticize being a missionary overseas and get caught up in the idea of living in a foreign country and sacrificing it all for the cause of Christ. He shared how men and women approach him about joining his missions team and seem "on fire" for the Lord—until he asks them, "Tell me about your ministry at home." In other words…do your neighbors know that you are a Christian? OUCH! What he was saying was simple. If you are not sharing Christ at home, what makes you think you will do it overseas? If you are not serving at home, what makes you think you will serve abroad?

You don't have to be in church long before you hear phrases like "He doesn't call the equip …He equips the called." Or "God won't ask you to do what He won't prepare you to do." They are clichés, but there is truth in both statements. The Bible is a source of truth for any issue we will face, including evangelism and serving broken people. As we strive to be women used by God, we must remember the model that was set for us.

> "But you will receive power when the Holy Spirit comes on you; and you will be my witnesses in Jerusalem, and in all Judea and Samaria, and to the ends of the earth."
>
> *Acts 1:8, NIV*

I am not a seminary graduate and have not studied commentaries on that passage. But here is my heartfelt analogy of that passage. I believe Jesus is saying two things: go...and go wider. What if Jerusalem was your family and friends? What if you went wider and Judea became your neighbors and co-workers? What if you went even wider and Samaria became everyone else?

This is the way that I am prayerfully choosing to model my service to Christ and through Him...the world. Is this beginning to make you a little uncomfortable? Are doubts beginning to flood your mind? Oh, wouldn't Satan love to discourage you with fear and apprehension? Many of you will begin to think of reasons why you can only impact one arena. Your to-do list is long and your energy level is low. Relax...breathe...but don't think you are off the hook. I truly believe everyone from the young mom raising toddlers to the retired woman can fit this into her lifestyle. No excuses! It's not about sacrificing family and responsibilities. It's about changing our mindset.

To navigate our way through this let's think about two groups, those we would invite inside our home like friends and family and those who are not quite as close. Let's start with those closest to us.

Why do we struggle in this area?? I have a theory and it isn't based on any scientific explanation or any deep-rooted theology. It's based on personal experience. I love sharing the Gospel. I crave opportunities to share the greatest love story with others but I haven't always been faithful with certain audiences. I love standing before 300 women and proclaiming the name of Jesus, but there was a time in my life when I would break into a sweat at the thought of sharing my testimony with a member of my family. Sounds strange! Why would I fear giving life-changing and life-saving information to the people I love most?

I think we find it easier to skip over our close circle of friends and family because of the fear of inadequacy, rejection and judgment. If they reject us or ridicule us the hurt is deep. But if a stranger dismisses us, they are still just a stranger.

Our family and friends also know us better than anyone else. I will never forget December 6, 2010. That is the day I sat by my dad's bedside holding his hand as he gently slipped into eternity. I remember watching his shallow breathing and realizing soon he would be in the presence of Jesus. I wasn't sure how much time he had, but I knew it wasn't much. For the first time in *YEARS* I told my dad I loved him. I know that he knew that I loved him, but I never said it audibly. I remember my mom climbing on to his hospital bed and caressing his hair. She told him how much she loved him and how much she appreciated the years they had together. It was a beautiful sight and we were both grateful for having that time with dad.

There was another profound moment that day. I sat by his bed in peace. I was sad about him dying but an unexplainable peace covered my soul. My dad's faith was in Jesus Christ so I knew this was just a temporary separation and someday I would see him in heaven. I realized how much I wanted that for my entire family. I want to know we will be together in heaven and it lit a fire in me to share the Gospel with them.

The first opportunity I took was at his funeral. I knew I could not make the decision for other people, but I wanted to know I had been obedient and seized the moment. At the holidays I felt another strong conviction to share Christ with a family member. I was SCARED. What would I say? What if she became defensive or angry? God reminded me of an important truth—sometimes obedience is hard and sometimes people will get angry but I can't save people…only Jesus can. My role is to share the Gospel and let the Holy Spirit do the rest.

Recently I was looking at the shelter's client roster and saw a name that looked very familiar. It was a mom with three young children who had come to the shelter a year ago in dire straits. The father of her children was in prison, and she was homeless and without resources. However, she was a model client who worked hard and quickly secured housing. She was accepted into one of the best programs in Akron for homeless moms. When I visited her apartment and dropped off Christmas presents, she was so proud of her new home and excited about her new start. I was disappointed to see that within a year she had lost that home.

I said hello to her and her precious children and asked her the question that was on my mind. "What happened?" She was honest and didn't try to sugar coat it or make excuses. She explained she had fallen back into some old habits and tried to reconcile with the man who landed her in the shelter the first time. Part of me wanted to say, "Don't you get it?" But I knew that was not my role and would do nothing but make her feel worse about her situation. All I could do was be kind and loving and offer her hope that maybe this time it would be different.

We often see this same scenario at the shelter; women get to a better place and then return to old habits. They enter the shelter with a much deeper issue then lack of housing. If we don't get to the root of the problem, we are just sending them out the same way they came in, only this time with a lease and a key. Months later, when they find themselves homeless again, it's frustrating, but we love them and start again. We can experience the same feelings when trying to share Christ with those closest to us. Often we tell them the "good news" and they continue to reject the message and us. Sometimes they are not ready. It doesn't mean that we don't stop trying.

Taking a stand for Christ can be lonely sometimes. It can open us up for ridicule and opposition. This should come as no surprise. Peter tells us to expect it!

> ... *If you suffer as a Christian, do not be ashamed, but praise God that you bear that name. For it is time for judgment to begin with the family of God; and if it begins with us, what will the outcome be for those who do not obey the gospel of God? And, "If it is hard for the righteous to be saved, what will become of the ungodly and the sinner?" So, then, those who suffer according to God's will should commit themselves to their faithful Creator and continue to do good.*
>
> 1 Peter 4:16-19, NIV

Let me introduce you to Jaclyn. Jaclyn was a stay-at-home mom in suburbia. Her neighborhood looked like a Hollywood movie set with white picket fences and mini-vans in the driveways. She connected with other neighborhood moms for conversation, support and occasional gossip. Across the street was a mom who also had a small child but was never invited to hang out with the other women. Why? Well, it seems her lifestyle was not like the others. She was living with her boyfriend and taking care of both his children from a previous relationship and the two they'd had together. In other words, she wasn't like them. Her family dynamic was different and a little out of the ordinary for this neighborhood.

At times it was easier for Jaclyn to follow the crowd and ignore the conviction God was placing on her heart. She was a Christian and she knew the restlessness inside her was the Holy Spirit moving her to reach out to this mom, no matter what the cost. One day as Jaclyn was outside with her children, the young mom came outside. Jaclyn knew this was the time to walk in obedience and reach out. Besides, the other moms were inside and would not be able to see her engaging the mom. She could be obedient to God and no one would know. The two women began to talk and before long neighbors were glancing across the street. Jaclyn began to feel awkward, wondering what the other moms thought of her. But it mattered more to her what God thought.

Two nights later during dinner there was a knock on the door. Standing in Jaclyn's doorway, in the middle of a thunderstorm, was her neighbor carrying her infant. She explained to Jaclyn that her boyfriend had become verbally abusive and she needed a place to go. She decided to come to her new friend's house across the street. After finding her some dry clothes and giving her a hot meal, Jaclyn began to talk with the woman about her situation. Hearing a prompting from the Holy Spirit, Jaclyn called another Christian friend and asked her to join them for coffee.

Over a cup of coffee, the Gospel was shared. That night the neighbor heard the good news of Jesus and accepted Him as her Lord and Savior. She began to attend Bible study at Jaclyn's church. She began to receive counsel from the church and received assistance as she moved from an abusive household to a safe place of her own. Her life was changed because Jaclyn walked across the street. Jaclyn overcame fear and endured judgment for the sake of the Gospel. I think it's worth it…don't you?

I was speaking at a women's conference on this very topic when the Lord prompted me to use the example of my father's illness. I shared how my dad was gravely ill and was in desperate need of a new liver. What if someone had the resources to help my dad and refused? How cruel it would be for someone to tell me, "I know where your dad can find the lifesaving organ he needs, but I refuse to tell you." We all agreed that it would be a helpless situation and one of extreme hurt and frustration. To know that someone could save my dad's life and to refuse would be hard to accept. I went on to explain that this is how we sometimes handle the Gospel—we have knowledge of a "life-giving" Savior but we refuse to share the good news because it's too hard, too uncomfortable or too frightening. We are withholding life-saving information when we say no to God.

After the session ended, a woman approached me. She asked if we could sit down and talk before she fainted. This made me very nervous! She began to cry and uttered words I never expected to hear: "I can save your dad's life." What? I began to cry and felt like I might faint, too! She went on to say she had recently gone to the doctor for an exam and was found to be in excellent health. The doctor commented on the size of her liver and explained she was a good candidate to donate part of her liver and not have her health affected. She wanted to be tested to see if she would be a good match for my dad.

To say I was speechless is an understatement. Here stood a precious woman who did not know me or my dad. But she knew Jesus and felt He was nudging her to provide life-saving information. She was being selfless, obedient and sacrificial. She was being like Christ. We sat there in total awe of what God had just done. Weeks after the conference we connected and she still felt compelled to help my dad. Unfortunately, a procedure of this type is very dangerous for the donor and my dad was too ill to receive a transplant.

A year later we ran into each other at the same conference. We recalled the experience and both agreed that God still used it to make a difference in our lives. We both knew that what God had in mind that day was not a healing for my dad but an act of obedience for her and for me. This woman had every reason to say no to God that day. She was scared, confused and no one would have ever known. But her priorities were in order and she made it all about God. Let's do the same!

DISCUSSION QUESTIONS:

1. Have you ever shared the gospel with anyone? Write down that story. If not, what has held you back? (Examples: inadequacy, fear, rejection.) How can you overcome it?

2. Joy talks about her struggle to share Christ with those closest to her, including members of her own family. Have you had similar experiences? Why do you think it is easier for us to talk to strangers about our faith that those who know and love us best?

3. Read Matthew 10:32-33 and James 1:22. How do these verses spur you to bring the gospel home?

CHAPTER NINE

UNCOVERING YOUR ONE

In chapter eight I addressed our service in Jerusalem, which represented our close inner circle. Are you ready to travel a little further and explore Judea and Samaria? No passport needed, just an obedient heart and attitude.

I recently attended a woman's conference that dedicated an entire area for ministries to showcase their cause. The orphan booth grabbed my heart with pictures of children in dire need of a home. The sex-trafficking booth made me angry when I heard the stories of young girls being abused and exploited. The youth ministry booth made my heart heavy for the obstacles teens face today and the difficulties of peer pressure and negative influences. Each one affected me in a different way and each one made an impact. However, it would be unrealistic for me to invest in all of them; each would get only a third of my attention and it would probably lead to frustration and burnout.

But what if I focused on the one passion…what if I was blessed to know exactly what my Judea/Samaria passion was? The passion or cause that goes beyond my family and friends and causes me to look beyond the familiar and safe? I am sure my family and friends tire of me talking about the clients at the shelter but when you are passionate about a cause, it is sometimes hard to stay silent. The homeless population is my ONE.

What if we each found our ONE? I believe we could make a HUGE impact if we each committed ourselves to one cause or one person. In other words…what if we each chose to walk parallel with a cause or person? Here is an example of what I mean by that phrase. You find yourself part of a women's Bible study and a prayer request has been brought up by a woman who is possibly struggling with infertility. In your past you struggled with the same issue. This woman is crying out to God asking for answers and is feeling hopeless, a sentiment that you remember all too well. You begin to feel a restless feeling and a prompting to reach out to her. The prompting is from the Holy Spirit and you now have a choice…say yes or no. Saying yes is obedient…saying no is a sin. Reaching out to this woman and offering encouragement, prayer and maybe counsel is an example of walking parallel. You are not walking ahead by telling her what to do. You are not walking behind by refusing to help. You are walking beside her…you are walking parallel to her. You weren't prompted to sacrifice your family for her. You were being asked to be available and obedient.

We can find many stories of modern-day women walking "parallel" with others, but some of the greatest examples are from scripture.

> *At that time Mary got ready and hurried to a town in the hill country of Judea, where she entered Zechariah's home and greeted Elizabeth. When Elizabeth heard Mary's greeting, the baby leaped in her womb,*

and Elizabeth was filled with the Holy Spirit. In a loud voice she exclaimed: "Blessed are you among women, and blessed is the child you will bear! But why am I so favored, that the mother of my Lord should come to me? As soon as the sound of your greeting reached my ears, the baby in my womb leaped for joy. Blessed is she who has believed that the Lord would fulfill his promises to her!"

Luke 1:39-45, NIV

I love this story! What a great example of women helping other women! Can you imagine what is going through Mary's mind? She is about to experience one of life's biggest moments—the birth of her first child—and she's the only woman in history who got there through the work of the Holy Spirit. But Mary knew who she could go to. She knew that not only would Elizabeth understand pregnancy, she would also understand and accept the unusual circumstances. While others could have judged her and turned the situation into "water well gossip," Mary had someone she could trust. Do you? Are you someone another woman can trust?

The Old Testament story of Naomi and Ruth is another great example of women walking parallel.

When she heard in Moab that the LORD had come to the aid of his people by providing food for them, Naomi and her daughters-in-law prepared to return home from there. With her two daughters-in-law she left the place where she had been living and set out on the road that would take them back to the land of Judah.

Then Naomi said to her two daughters-in-law, "Go back, each of you, to your mother's home. May the LORD show kindness to you, as you have shown to your dead and to me. May the LORD grant that each of you will find rest in the home of another husband."

Then she kissed them and they wept aloud and said to her, "We will go back with you to your people."

But Naomi said, "Return home, my daughters. Why would you come with me? Am I going to have any more sons, who could become your husbands? Return home, my daughters; I am too old to have another husband. Even if I thought there was still hope for me—even if I had a husband tonight and then gave birth to sons—would you wait until they grew up? Would you remain unmarried for them? No, my daughters. It is more bitter for me than for you, because the LORD's hand has gone out against me!"

At this they wept again. Then Orpah kissed her mother-in-law good-by, but Ruth clung to her.

"Look," said Naomi, "your sister-in-law is going back to her people and her gods. Go back with her."

But Ruth replied, "Don't urge me to leave you or to turn back from you. Where you go I will go, and where you stay I will stay. Your people will be my people and your God my God. Where you die I will die, and there I will *be buried. May the LORD deal with me, be it ever so severely, if anything but death separates you and me." When Naomi realized that Ruth was determined to go with her, she stopped urging her.*

Ruth 1:6-18, NIV

This was a difficult, inconvenient situation for Ruth, but she knew what God was calling her to do. It was not about it being easy....it was about being obedient, faithful and supportive.

I wonder why this issue is something that doesn't come naturally to us. As women, we are considered to be nurturers, but why does taking the time to help take such effort? As a woman I wish that I could say that most of the time we do a good job of this, but it seems we fail many times. It seems that it is easier for us to let slander and malice fall off our tongues rather than encouragement and affirmations. I am amazed at how young this begins to surface. Little girls as young as preschoolers begin to bully or taunt and it continues through school. Girls are left out of social circles and bullying begins to have a huge impact on self-esteem. I often counsel my daughters that a bully is just a girl with a void in her life and that void is God-shaped. Bullying is the polar opposite of walking parallel. It seems that we are seeing this more and more but "mean girls" existed in the Bible.

There was a certain man from Ramathaim, a Zuphite from the hill country of Ephraim, whose name was Elkanah son of Jeroham, the son of Elihu, the son of Tohu, the son of Zuph, an Ephraimite. He had two wives; one was called Hannah and the other Peninnah. Peninnah had children, but Hannah had none.

> *Year after year this man went up from his town to worship and sacrifice to the LORD Almighty at Shiloh, where Hophni and Phinehas, the two sons of Eli, were priests of the LORD. Whenever the day came for Elkanah to sacrifice, he would give portions of the meat to his wife Peninnah and to all her sons and daughters. But to Hannah he gave a double portion because he loved her, and the LORD had closed her womb. Because the LORD had closed Hannah's womb, her rival kept provoking her in order to irritate her. This went on year after year. Whenever Hannah went up to the house of the LORD, her rival provoked her till she wept and would not eat. Her husband Elkanah would say to her, "Hannah, why are you weeping? Why don't you eat? Why are you downhearted? Don't I mean more to you than ten sons?"*
>
> 1 Samuel 1:1-8, NIV

Elkanah was a man with two wives. One was named Hannah and the other was Peninnah. Peninnah was able to give Elkanah children but Hannah could not. Hannah struggled with fertility and felt great shame. Hannah was feeling the sadness and emptiness that many women feel today. Not only did Hannah have to deal with her fertility issues, she was taunted by Peninnah. What is the value of being a Peninnah?

Are you ready to adjust your mindset and find your ONE? Are you ready to make it more than a project but a way of living? Are you ready to start walking parallel? Think of it as a journey and one that is not meant be done alone. There is no a shortage of causes and individuals that need you. Scripture is clear that "the harvest is plenty but the workers are few." God will direct your path and lead you to where He wants you to serve. There is not a clearinghouse for causes...it is a conversation between you and God.

Another example might be if you are sitting in church listening to someone speak about the orphan situation in third world countries. Usually your mind is wandering and you dismiss the cause as just another project in search of your time, talent or treasure, but this time it is different. As the presentation ends, your thoughts continue. You can't seem to shake the feeling of needing to do something. It's not just a desire to do a good deed but more like anger for the injustice of the situation. You begin to think of ways that you could possibly help. You are now CAUGHT! There is now a need that has your name on it. Congratulations...you have now found your ONE. You will know it when you find it. It will consume your thoughts. It will energize you. It will anger you and excite you at the same time. You will begin to see your talents matching up with the cause. You will begin to see that the cause needs you. You will begin to see you were made for this.

Let me introduce you to Mandy Young. Mandy Young has a contagious enthusiasm, a zest for the Lord and for life. You probably know a woman you would describe the same way, but there is something different about Mandy. Mandy is the only person in the world with her medical condition.

For years Mandy and her family traveled all over the country begging doctors to find out why she continued to experience life-threatening infections. Finally, when Mandy was eight, a clinic in Northern Virginia was able to offer Mandy and her family a definite diagnosis: Clostridia Septicemia secondary to

Gas Gangrene. The combination of these had not been seen since WWII. As the infection consumed her body it was necessary to amputate her left leg and hip to save her life. Mandy will spend the rest of her life battling this disease but it doesn't stop her from doing what God has called her to do. The quote below will give you an idea of Mandy's heart:

> *"I know God gave me my disease for a reason; it's not for my purpose, but for HIS. My life is not about me; unlike what my generation so wants us to believe, it's about HIM! And knowing that HE is in charge of my life gives me hope for those things that seem so unclear, like my disease and living without answers for so many years."*

Mandy now spends her time reaching out to others who have had to face amputation. She can sincerely say to them, "I know what you are going through." They can look at Mandy and see hope. They can see someone who faced a specific obstacle and overcame it. Mandy is living a very productive life and faces her challenges head-on. She loves sharing her story and welcomes questions like, "What happened to your leg?" and "What do you do with your left shoes?" Not only does Mandy use her story to inspire others, she uses her story to share Christ. Mandy found her ONE!

When I was in college, I was undecided about a major and felt pressured to declare my area of study. I became envious of the people who seemed to know exactly what they wanted to do. I knew I liked to argue and prove my point so I became a political science major so I could go to law school. A few months later

I began to feel a call to serve so I decided for a brief moment to consider nursing....and then business...you get the picture? I never took the time to really seek direction as to my major. This resulted in many extra years of college and unnecessary student loans.

I look back now and realize there were signs from the beginning about the direction I should have taken. When I was a sophomore in college I was one of the rare students who loved speech class. I always volunteered to do my speech first and I loved doing it. The following year I received an internship with IBM; one of my responsibilities was to train businesses to use their copier. (Okay...stop laughing...those machines can be complicated.) I loved teaching in front of groups and speaking about the machine. I never had a fear of speaking in front of people. Today I still love it and I'm blessed to have opportunities to speak at several events each year. Some are for the homeless shelter and others are for ministry reasons. As I look back on the journey that brought me to where I am today, I see that it wasn't always a smooth road. At times there was self-doubt, lack of confidence and enormous spiritual battles. Many times I thought about silencing my voice and God would quickly remind me that I was His and He created me for this purpose. He continues to "complete the work that was started" within me.

I was blessed to be raised in a family where this was and still is modeled to me on a continual basis.

My mom, a breast cancer survivor, has some sort of radar that detects other women battling this disease. At the mere sight of a pink ribbon she immediately forms a sisterhood and she is constantly reaching out to women who are walking the journey of breast cancer. Mom is a role model to others as someone who has fought the battle and won. Her ONE is being an advocate for breast cancer. My sister Pattie has a passion for special needs children. She is drawn to children with Down Syndrome and loves being involved in their lives. God placed her in a high school and she is an advocate for the underdog. My sister Debbie is a nurse and knew from a young age that it was a call on her life. I love that members of my family have found their ONE.

I could fill this chapter with stories of other women who have found their ONE.

ACCESS came to be because a group of people had a passion for homeless women and children. In 1984 they saw a void—there was no safe place in the community for homeless women and children to live. There was a need and they satisfied the need. There was a problem and they found the solution. Fast forward 27 years and none of the original founders are part of the organization—not because they quit, but because they introduced this need to other committed workers through the years who also caught the vision. I wonder what would have happened if that original group had found themselves too busy or too unavailable to help. I am glad that I never have to worry about the answer to that question and thousands of women and children are as well.

A day will come when our help won't be needed and we can enjoy a life of peace and joy. Homeless shelters won't exist, "orphanage" will be a foreign term and sadness and brokenness will be obsolete. What a glorious day that will be...but it's not here yet. Until that day comes, let's exhaust ourselves for the cause of Christ. Let's find our ONE!

DISCUSSION QUESTIONS:

1. What does Joy mean when she says "we must each find our ONE"? Do you know what your "ONE" is yet? Explain.

2. Have you had the experience of "walking parallel" with someone? Reread the examples in this chapter as well as the stories of Mary & Elizabeth and Ruth & Naomi. Write down and be ready to share your own story.

CHAPTER TEN

UNCOVERING YOUR MISSIONAL ENTOURAGE

Last night, in the comfort of my own home and wearing my favorite flannel pajamas (bet you are jealous of my glamorous life!), I sat and watched the stars of Hollywood walk the red carpet. Women were dressed in beautiful gowns and had flawless hair and perfect make-up. It was fun to watch their "handlers" walk a few steps behind or in front of them, clearing the way as the actress navigated her fish-tail skirt in 6-inch stilettos. Commentators asked the women how long it took them to get ready. It was clear it "took a village" to prepare them for this night. It wasn't your average woman preparing for an elegant event. It required a stylist, publicist, agent, manager, manicurist, hair stylist and probably even a therapist to prepare for the evening. In other words…it required an entourage.

I often watch the award shows and daydream what it would be like to have an entourage, a group that would include someone to do my hair, make-up, and wardrobe. It would be great to have someone do the things for me I don't enjoy. On my own it takes two minutes to do my make-up and 30 seconds to pull my hair into a ponytail. I would love to have that "just got my hair done at a salon" feeling every day.

I also wonder what the movie stars would look like if they had to go it alone. Their publicist promotes their careers, while their managers work out the details and their agents secure their bookings. Having others to take care of the details allows them to spend most of their energy on doing what they do best… act.

You need a missional entourage. As you begin to put legs to what you have learned from this book, you will need help. You will need to surround yourself with people who will help you be successful. I consider myself a dreamer; I have always been unafraid to try new things and take a risk. I will get an idea and my first response is to share it with someone, but I'm strategic in who I tell. One of my "entourage" members is a person who will help me process the idea and think through the needed steps. If the idea is crazy or stupid, they ask questions and help me come to this conclusion on my own. The other person is my mom. She supports everything I do and never tries to stop me from following a dream.

On the other hand, there is one type of person that I never share my dreams with—the person who hates everything and believes risks are for the young. They are the ones who refuse to leave their comfort zone and take huge leaps of faith. We all have them in our lives…the perpetual naysayers. I love them… but I don't invite them to be part of my missional entourage.

During Christmas of 2009, I experienced the importance of surrounding myself with these encouragers and supporters. Our family was at the Christmas Eve service, enjoying the music and the message. The pastor talked about the inn keeper, and how this character in the story sometimes gets a bad rap for giving

Mary and Joseph a stable and a manger. The pastor explained the innkeeper actually gave what he had to give. The challenge was for each of us to give from what God has given us, no matter the size or the amount.

At that moment God began asking me what I could give on this Christmas Eve. It became very clear He was asking me to do something that would seem weird to many. He was asking our family to sacrifice our Christmas Eve tradition and serve. Instead of going home and opening the traditional Christmas Eve presents, He was asking us to do something different. Specifically, we were to go and pick up sandwiches and hot chocolate. Yes…it was that specific. I can't explain it, but God was asking us to take the food and drink to a very specific location. As we loaded into the car after the service, I was nervous about sharing this news with my family and to the children who were chomping at the bit to open presents. God quickly reminded me that I was surrounded by like-minded people.

But when I shared my idea, no one complained or questioned what I was saying, and that night God led us to people who needed help. It was nothing short of a supernatural and God-ordained experience. It felt AMAZING to be the hands and feet of God on that Christmas Eve.

When I began feeling called to write this book, I knew exactly who to tell and who not to tell. It was scary; I was putting myself in a vulnerable spot and the least bit of negativity would keep me from following through. Knowing the spiritual battle that was going to take place, I formed a prayer team. As discouragement and doubt reared its ugly head, I contacted these 17 prayer warriors who approached the throne of God on my behalf. They played a huge part in writing this book. Your missional entourage must include people who have a burden for prayer. Don't go at this alone! Surround yourself with those who are like-minded and prayer-minded.

As you build your missional entourage, partner with others who are gifted differently from you. In a previous chapter I mentioned the group of 12 women who volunteered at the shelter. Twelve women had come together for a common goal. Their goal was to serve others the way Christ had called them to serve. They were like-minded and shared a common goal and passion. As they prayerfully formed this group, they didn't put an ad in the church bulletin, or post an invite on Facebook. God had already brought the ladies together through their interest in reading a book. There was already a common foundation to build on. The conviction was so strong and they knew that they could not go back to their old lives. They knew that they had to take this new-found passion and put it to good use. After completing the project, this group still remains. The entourage is still together.

I believe we were made to crave community. The Bible includes many examples of like-minded individuals coming together for a common cause. When God called Noah to build an outrageous boat, his family rallied around him and provided support. When Esther received her mission from God, she asked others to pray for her and become a support system for her. There were three men in that furnace, not one. We were designed to do things together. I love being part of a team and not trying to do the impossible on my own. When I'm hurting I want others to surround me and when I am rejoicing I do not want to celebrate alone.

Lastly, but most importantly, make sure you are in constant communion with the One who gives you the opportunities and the one who deserves all the glory and praise. Compassion and obedience can seem unattainable and impossible. But as the head of your missional entourage, God has made clear His commitment to you.

> *Never will I leave you; never will I forsake you.*
> *Hebrews 13:5, NIV*

> *....And surely I am with you always, to the very end of the age.*
> *Matthew 28:20, NIV*

As I was wrapping up the writing of this book, I began to wonder if this was all in vain. Do women even *want* to walk alongside each other, and will women be open to this concept? On a whim I posted on Facebook, "What is something you would like to learn from another woman?" I began to immediately receive responses. One lady wanted wisdom in raising teenage boys. Another wanted affirmation that beauty was not defined by her dress size or a number on a scale. A mom wanted someone to encourage her as she raises a tween in a materialistic world. Another dear woman expressed how great it was to have a mentor who encouraged her on her spiritual journey. In just a few moments, a community of women came together through a computer.

My prayer is that this book is a catalyst for change in your life. I pray it ignites a passion for serving others and inspires a new way of thinking. I hope that showing compassion to "the least of these" becomes as natural as breathing, that reaching out to someone in need becomes a natural habit and doesn't cause a whip-lash. May your eyes be constantly open for opportunities to serve and give back.

Be like the innkeeper and give from what you have. It doesn't have to be perfect and it doesn't have to be a lot. It just has to come from a sincere heart. Remember the widow and her offering described in the scriptures:

> *Jesus sat down opposite the place where the offerings were put and watched the crowd putting their money into the temple treasury. Many rich people threw in large amounts. But a poor widow came and put in two very small copper coins, worth only a fraction of a penny. Calling his disciples to him, Jesus said, "I tell you the truth, this poor widow has put more into the treasury than all the others. They all gave out of their wealth; but she, out of her poverty, put in everything—all she had to live on."*
>
> Mark 12: 41-44, NIV

As you begin this journey you will experience frustration, doubt and hesitancy. Don't quit! Don't stop! Your entourage is waiting to support you and your heavenly Father is there to give you everything you need. May God continue to reveal to you your ONE and may you run toward your purpose with zeal and strength. What are you waiting for?

DISCUSSION QUESTIONS:

1. What do you think of Joy's idea of having a "missional entourage"? Name some people you would include in yours and why they would be helpful to you.

2. Reread the story of the widow's offering in Mark 12:41-44. How does this encourage you to give, serve and love right now with what you have?

3. Name three things you will do as a result of reading this book. Share these with your "missional entourage" and let them keep you accountable!

STORIES OF PASSION

I believe we all have a dream or passion inside us. Some allow it to lie dormant while others are ready to dive in and live it out. Sometimes the first step is telling someone. The following amazing people are ready to share the passion God has placed on their hearts. Read their stories, add them to your prayer list, and let them inspire you to dream.

RUTH RIDLEY
dear friend and mentor

Ruth has a passion for marriage—not just a good marriage, or even a great marriage, but the marriage God designed. If you asked Ruth to prioritize her life she would say, "God, my husband, my family, then others." Our culture would be shocked to hear anyone put anything in front of the children, but Ruth knows this is exactly what God wants. The following excerpt, taken from an interview with Ruth, describes the motive behind her conviction.

> *If I were to write a book, it would be titled "My Husband Is More Than a Sperm Donor." My passion is for the husband/wife relationship, especially after the kids arrive. What kids want and need most is for their parents to love each other, and to be the foundation of their security. That love should be modeled daily, by making time for each other, complimenting each other and NOT being ships in the night.*
>
> *Keep your relationship current! Having raised four wonderful kids, I do realize it is not easy, but it's the best investment you will make. We went through the "empty nest" and the heartache of letting go of the kids, but because we kept our relationship current we had a foundation to build on after the kids grew up.*
>
> *And for those of you haven't gone through that yet, there is life on the other side of the mountain and it is mar-*

velous!!! God has affirmed this passion every day as I see a smile on my husband's face when I take him a cup of tea or compliment him. No, I am not as consistent as I could be; I am a work in progress.

Ruth reminds us that steps to improve our marriages can come in all sizes. Small gestures such as an encouraging word or refusing to be on the phone while you are together can make a huge difference. Ruth has a passion for sharing this with other women and is praying for God to make the next steps clear. She earnestly prays for the marriages surrounding her and is always open to opportunities God gives her to mentor women in this area.

AMY RIDLEY
friend and soon-to-be first-time mommy

You don't have to be around Amy very long before you realize two things: she has a passion for Jesus and she has a passion for teenage girls. For Amy, it is a great day when those two passions collide. Discipling young women and seeing them come to a closer and more intimate relationship with Jesus energizes Amy. This passion was ignited when Amy was in college and a family friend came to Christ. The friend was searching for guidance in her new walk, and what began as a friendship quickly turned into discipleship and accountability. A new convert was growing and a long-time Christ follower was falling more in love with Jesus though this relationship as well.

Seven years later, Amy devotes as much time as she can to teenage girls and their spiritual growth. She meets regularly with girls and leads a Bible study every other week. She knows the importance of meeting them "where they are" and loving them with grace and mercy. God affirmed this passion by equipping Amy with the gifts needed to be effective. We are not all called to work with teens...Amy is!

Amy's dream for this ministry is that the girls would grow in their relationship with Christ and start discipling other girls and keep spreading His love. Anyone involved in ministry knows how hard it can be sometimes to stay motivated. I asked Amy what keeps this passion alive and how God affirmed this calling. "It's all about the relationship," she replied, "and seeing God work in their lives.

Amy is a great example of what it looks like to say "YES" to God.

LEIGH GREY
friend, speaker and former ministry partner

I have often heard people complain about the Internet being a waste of time. Well, that's where I met Leigh and my life has been blessed immensely! I began reading her blog and was blown away by her humor, authenticity and heart for Jesus. She is passionate about sharing the good news of Jesus with anyone who will listen...and they listen! She is also passionate about discipleship. Leigh uses her gift of speaking to share how exciting it is to follow Christ. As she so wonderfully says, "Living for Him is not a drag, but can be done triumphantly with joy! Developing a daily walk with Him is about living in His presence, not living life and mentioning His presence."

Leigh's passion was ignited through her former youth pastor, Ergun Caner. Caner, a converted Muslim, showed Leigh how "real and vibrant the Word of God was and that it can bring much joy through any circumstances," she shares.

Leigh is a gifted speaker and storyteller. She gives God credit for this gift and realized the calling while in junior high when He called her to "speak to many." Leigh speaks full time in the United States and around the world. Sometimes she may be sharing Jesus with hundreds of women or teens, sometimes to the 30 to 45 students who meet at her house each week. Leigh is always searching for new avenues to share the Gospel including Facebook, Twitter and her personal blog.

I love that Leigh is a fellow dreamer so I asked her what her biggest dream was for her ministry. "A TV show," she replied. I have no doubt that as Leigh partners with God, we will someday see that show, one that brings glory to our Lord and furthers His kingdom. The verses that spur her on and affirm her in ministry are as follows:

> *The Sovereign LORD has given me an instructed tongue, to know the word that sustains the weary. He wakens me morning by morning, wakens my ear to listen like one being taught. The Sovereign LORD has opened my ears, and I have not been rebellious; I have not drawn back.*
>
> *Isaiah 50:4-5, NIV*

> *For the eyes of the LORD range throughout the earth to strengthen those whose hearts are fully committed to him.*
>
> 2 Chronicles 16:9a, NIV

Leigh has passion...and God has a plan! What a great mix.

JENNI JACQUET PUSTINGER
friend, former classmate, everyday missionary

If you asked Jenni to describe her life, one word would stand out: BLESSED! Many of us would use the same word, but after reading Jenni's story, I soon realized she really knew what BLESSED meant. To Jenni, blessing does not mean material accumulation or financial windfalls. It is more about the favor of the Lord. Unlike some of the other women profiled here, Jenni's passion is not a specific task but more a way of living. Her passion is to simply be used by God in the everyday, to always "be in the now" and stay open to spontaneous serving. I was touched by Jenni's humility as she shared her adventures in mission and how she looks for opportunities to minister to the needs of others in the everyday. Being mission-oriented doesn't have to always be planned and with an agenda or schedule.

During a recent trip to Belize, the purpose was to build homes, but Jenni realized her team could do more. As a mom, she wondered why the families did not have photos in their homes. Although she's not a trained photographer, she took family portraits and gave the families this special gift.

From the view of an outsider, one would say Jenni is doing great things for God. But Jenni's passion is not to please the world, but to please God. It can't be defined by a strategic plan or mission trip agenda. It is simply to be obedient to God and to be real, relevant and ready each day!

In closing, I wanted to share with you two verses that Jenni shared in her interview.

> *But the one who does not know and does things deserving punishment will be beaten with few blows. From everyone who has been given much, much will be demanded; and from the one who has been entrusted with much, much more will be asked.*
> *Luke 12:48, NIV*

> *What good is it, my brothers, if a man claims to have faith but has no deeds? Can such faith save him?*
> *James 2:14, NIV*